It Was Their War Too:
Canadian Women
and
World War I

Pat Staton

Green Dragon Press
Toronto

It Was Their War Too:
Canadian Women and World War I

Pat Staton

© 2006
Green Dragon Press
2267 Lakeshore Blvd. West, #1009
Toronto, ON M8V 3X2
Tel: 416 251 6366

Cover art: Pat Staton - Maelstrom
Cover design: Ermanno Biot

Cover photos: From the top: Teacher Winnifred Cassel and friends working on the farm (courtesy Winnifred Cassel); Charlotte Edith Anderson Monture (Photo: John Moses); Grace MacPherson as a Voluntary Aid Detachment (VAD) (Library and Archives Canada/Department of National Defence Collection/PA-001305); Women Munitions Workers (Library and Archives Canada/Department of National Defence Collection/PA-024639); Nursing Sister Ruby Gordon Peterkin, 1916 (Library and Archives Canada/ACC. No.1970-163/e002283118.)

Design/layout: Ermanno Biot represented by Erica Alexander, contact: ericaealexander@hotmail.com

Library and Archives Canada Cataloguing in Publication

Staton, Pat, 1933-
It was their war too: Canadian women and World War one / Pat Staton

Includes bibliographical references.
ISBN 1-896781-16-0

1.World War, 1914-1918—Women—Canada. 2. World War, 1914-1918--War Work—Canada, 3. Women--Canada—History--20th century. I. Title.

D639.W7S73 2006   940.3'0820971   C2006-901591-0

Table of Contents

GREEN DRAGON PRESS

GREEN DRAGON PRESS

Foreword

Most accounts of the 1914-18 war, commonly referred to afterward as the "Great War," the "war to end all wars," as though such a disaster could or would ever be repeated, focus on the political causes and horrifying loss of life in the bombings and trench warfare. The aftermath is usually described in terms of the Paris Peace Conference in 1919 and the devastation wrought by the worldwide flu epidemic, which added to the death toll. The contributions of, and consequences for, women's participation in the war effort are not well documented. A number of published diaries of nursing sisters who saw service on the battlefields in France (see Bongard, Gass) and the National Film Board "And We Knew How to Dance" do provide some details of the daily lives of these courageous women. The objective of this book is to bring together documents, posters, photographs, diaries, short essays and brief biographies to present the range of experiences of Canadian women. The Great War changed the lives of Canadian women as well as the men. The lives of those men who did return from war service were forever altered and they returned to a changed society. But women's lives were changed as well. Their organizational experience had stood them in good stead; they gained new job skills and many, although not all, women gained the vote.

Women, having learned to operate factory machinery, make financial decisions and run farms, small businesses and homes on their own, did not react positively to calls to return to their pre-war roles. There was a new sense of freedom in the air, characterized by simpler, more comfortable clothes, new music and new job opportunities. There would be no return to the confining Edwardian dress, all-male professions and restrictions on political participation. Though pressure was applied for women to give up their jobs to homecoming servicemen and return to their '"natural" places as the keepers of the hearth, many women refused to do so, and indeed the huge loss of life on the battlefields of Europe and in the flu epidemic meant that marriage and motherhood were closed for many women. A generation of men was lost and so women turned willingly or unwillingly to other options.

This book is dedicated to the memory of Robert Thomas Staton
1932 – 2004
Husband, father, grandfather, feminist, friend

❦

GREEN DRAGON PRESS

Working Girl : " Mr. Eaton, can't you please make life a little easier for us ? "

The long working hours of women shop clerks was the subject of many letters and cartoons in both mainstream and community newspapers. This illustration, which appeared in the March 2nd, 1912 edition of Jack Canuck ("a weekly review of what the public say, do and think") shows a working girl appealing to dry goods merchant Timothy Eaton to "make life a little easier for us."

Prelude

The period before World War I saw great changes in Canadian society. Rural populations moved to the factories and commerce of the cities. Between 1896 and 1912, two to three million people immigrated to this country, most of them European and white since official government policy made it almost impossible for Asians and Blacks to come here. In that same period, for example, fewer than a thousand of those immigrants were Black.

Urban growth brought unheard-of opportunities as well as new social problems. Agitation for workers' rights continued. And the movement for women's rights to education and the vote gathered even more momentum than it had over the previous decades.

Since the late 1870s, North America had been experiencing the birth of a reform movement – the first stage of feminism. Thousands of middle-class women became involved as volunteers with the creation of parks and recreation programs for children and improving public health. Women also became involved with the temperance movement, which advocated the prohibition of alcohol, because it was seen as a threat to the stability of the family. While their main objective was not votes for women, they soon realized voting was a way to achieve the desired changes by making their voices heard through the democratic process. Across the country, women mobilized to advocate for the right to vote. But discussion about women's "proper sphere" continued. A 1914 headline in the *Albertan* asked rhetorically, "Should women interfere in Civic Life?" The article led with this line: "What is woman's sphere and woman's work?

Should woman take any part in the outside world?" It went on to report on a debate of the local council executive, where a councilor warned that: "The women of today are shirking their proper responsibilities and the day would come when the men would have to cook the meals, while the women were out legislating."

In any event women were not "out legislating" but they were taking on new roles
It has been estimated that during the period just prior to and after the turn of the twentieth century, nine out of every ten women in Canada belonged to some kind of organization. Through their political and social activities, and sometimes through the men they knew, these organizations provided women's main access to political power. Power and influence, however limited, were far more available to white middle-class women than to Black, Aboriginal, working class or immigrant women. A large number of national voluntary philanthropic and religious organizations developed in the late 1980s, including inter-denominational groups like the Women's Christian Temperance Union (WCTU), cultural organizations like the Women's Art Association of Canada, and purely charitable societies. Now they began to organize as women around women's issues.

Women took the skills they had developed at home, at church and in the collective sharing of work in the early days of the country and applied them to organizing for the vote, for prohibition, which they felt would solve the social problems of the family, poverty and disease, and for justice for women in the workplace.

GREEN DRAGON PRESS

The events they organized included carrying suffrage banners in Labour Day and Dominion Day parades, organizing local meetings such as the 1896 gathering of seven women teachers that launched the Toronto Women Teachers' Association, a founding association of the Federation of Women Teachers' Associations of Ontario (FWTAO), and impressive, well organized demonstrations like the one in 1909 by the Canadian Suffrage Association, the powerful Women's Christian Temperance Union and hundreds of members from 14 suffrage societies. One thousand women marched to the Ontario Legislature. A petition of 100,000 names of people supporting suffrage was presented. The demonstration, its participants and the causes it represented were ignored.

Women organizers understood how to organize entertainment and use humour to make a point. One endeavour, repeated with good effect several times, was the Mock Parliament. The first, staged in Winnipeg in 1893 by Dr. Amelia Yeomans, journalist E. Cora Hind and Mrs. J. A. McClung, a temperance advocate who was the future mother-in-law of Nellie McClung, featured women taking roles for and against suffrage. It got excellent media coverage. Three years later in 1896 a similar event organized in Toronto's Allen Gardens by the Dominion Women's Enfranchisement Association in co-operation with the Ontario W.C.T.U. attracted attention to the suffrage cause. Later, in 1914, the day after Manitoba Premier Roblin once again stated his opposition to votes for women, Nellie McClung and the Political Equality League staged a mock "Women's Parliament" in the Walker Theater in Winnipeg. It was such a success it was repeated twice to

sold-out audiences. The proceeds from the ticket sales financed the rest of the Manitoba "Votes for Women" campaign.

Men supporters were well represented in the audience and some took part in the play. Women played the parts of the Premier and MPPs and debated the pros and cons of granting men the vote, exposing the sanctimonious and contradictory arguments used by male politicians to deny female suffrage. They received a deputation of vote-seeking men pushing a wheelbarrow full of petitions. The Premier, played by McClung, congratulated the men on their "splendid appearance," but told them "man is made for something higher and better than voting."

GREEN DRAGON PRESS

"Men were made to support families. What is a home without a bank account? In this agricultural province, the man's place is the farm. Shall I call man away from the useful plough and barrow to talk loud on street corners about things which do not concern him? Politics unsettles men, and unsettled men mean unsettled bills—broken furniture, and broken vows—and divorce…. When you ask for the vote you are asking me to break up peaceful happy homes—to wreck innocent lives…

It may be that I am old-fashioned," she concluded. "I may be wrong. After all, men may be human. Perhaps the time will come when men may vote with women." And she assured them solemnly that "The man who pays the grocer rules the world." McClung was faithfully echoing the words and tone of Premier Roblin speaking to the suffragists the day before, and the crowd applauded wildly.

Satirical Post Card
Canadian Women's Movement
Archives/canadiennes du
mouvement des femmes.

THE CLUB WOMAN

'Mid a clatter of tea-cups and spoons
And an atmosphere suited for swoons,
The President hen
Rails at the men,
And talks of prisms and prunes.

A Club is all right in its place. Find the place.

GREEN DRAGON PRESS

MOCK PARLIAMENT

... AND ...

PROMENADE CONCERT

FOR THE BENEFIT OF THE

W. C. T. U. Building Fund

PAVILION

Tuesday February 18th, '96

❋

ASSISTED BY THE

- VERDI QUARTETTE -

MISS NORMA REYNOLDS, Directress

❋

- - D'ALESANDRO ORCHESTRA - -

PROGRAMME AT 7.45

❋

REFRESHMENTS ON THE EUROPEAN PLAN

NORTH-ELDER PRINT.

Programme

1. Overture............ ......" Vendetta," .... .Orchestra
2. Deputation from Men's Enfranchisement Association and Men's Christian Temperance Union.
3. March.... ...." Oriental Echo,"................ Orchestra
4. Evening Sitting, Mock Parliament
5. Waltz Song ...." Se Seran Rose," .... Ardi
   Miss Gertie Black.
   Violin Obligato by Miss Hilda Davis.
6. Polka......... ....Trilby.... ... . Orchestra
7. Quartette .... { (a) " Lady Mine Thy Casement Open......... Barnby
                  { (b) " Robin Adair," .... Arranged by Macy
   The Verdi Quartette.
   Miss Elda Idle, Soprano.   Miss Mima Lund, Contralto.
   Mr. H. C. Johnson, Tenor.   Mr. H. C. Stutchbury, Baritone.

❋

PROMENADE

1. March .... "The Honeymoon," .... Rosey
2. Valse Di Concert . ..." Lune de Miel," .... Waldteufel
3. Gavotte .... " Heart's Delight," .... Warren
4. Grand Selection.......... " Il Trovatore,".................. Verat
5. Russian Mazurka.......... " La Czarina,"................. Ganne
6. March .... " King Cotton," ... .Sousa
7. Gavotte .... " La Parisienne,"................ Wanner
8. Spanish Serenade.......... " La Paloma," ... . Balfour
9. Galop Di Concert .... " High Tide,". ...., ...Armstrong

1 ....
2 ....
3 ....
4 ....

In 1896 a Mock Parliament event organized in Toronto's Allen Gardens by the Dominion Women's Enfranchisement Association in co-operation with the Ontario W.C.T.U. attracted attention to the suffrage cause. The "Plan of Members' Seats" included in the programme for the event identified the women who participated as "members of Parliament."

A number of well-known women activists and educators participated, including Dr. Emily Howard Stowe, her daughter, Dr. Augusta Stowe Gullen, Ada Marean Hughes, and Leticia Youmans.

GREEN DRAGON PRESS

Plan of Members' Seats

Noxon, A. Brant	Abercrombie, W. Welland.		SPEAKER, HON. A. O. RUTHERFORD	Forster, M C. Perth	Allen, B. Lanark	
Savigny, A. G. Victoria, W.	Burwash, M. Ottawa.	Stowe, Hon. Dr. E. H. Oxford.	Clerk, H. Johnston	McDonell, M. Toronto, N.	Riches, S. Lennox	Harrington, L.C. Stormont
Redmond, M. A. Peterboro.	Stevens, Hon. H. Kingston.	Gullen, Hon. Dr. A. S. Brant.		Hunter, G. Dundas	Rose, C. M. Grenville	Brown, A. Muskoka
Vance, A. Nipissing.	Ford, Hon. E. A. Monck.	Hughes, Hon. A. M. Middlesex, W.	Asst. Clerk, M. J. Luke.	Parker A. Halton	Jackson, M. M. Addington	Henderson, O. Victoria, E.
Lelean, E. Waterloo.	Teskey, S. Ray. Northumberland.	Sims, Hon. A. Hamilton.		Biggs, S.E. Norfolk	Smith, M., B.E. Lincoln	Hilborn, S. Parry Sound
Summerfeldt, J. Simcoe.	Campbell, F. R. Huron.	Wiggins, Hon. L. E. Ontario.		Spence, S F. Prince Edward	Walker, H. Cardwell	Bowbeer, C. Carleton
Duff, A. J. Peel.	Yeigh, E. Algoma.	Doane, S. A. N. York.		Brown, M. A. Frontenac	Youmans, I. Lambton	Wrigley, G. Dufferin
Cook, C. Wellington	Forest, I. Glengarry.	Laing, M. R. N. Middlesex.		Sanderson, A. Bruce, N.	Chamberlain, A. J. Elgin	Faircloth, L. S. Bruce S.
Cowan, A. M. Kent.	Ward, F. C. S. York.	Rose, J. M. Essex.	J. Semple, Sergt.-at-Arms	Orr, W. H. Stormont	Coad, E. Wentworth	Mason, W. Leeds

Illustrations courtesy Moira Armour.

Although large influential national women's organizations did not include Black women, they organized too. Wives of Black railroad workers founded the Coloured Women's Club of Montreal in 1902. The aim of the club was to bring attention to the problems faced by Blacks in Montreal, especially racial discrimination. They also assisted newly arrived Black immigrants. Bee Allen remembers the Eureka Club:

"The Eureka Club was founded in 1910. I always remembered that mother said that they had twenty members, and my mother was president of it for one year. They sent out mail and things like that, did little kindnesses. They were a social club when they first were formed, and they were very proud of the fact it wasn't too long before they all sat back and said we ought to be doing something worthwhile and there were many things they did. For instance, they sent Christmas baskets to the needy, and that grew into quite a thing."

No Burden to Carry: Narratives of Black Working Women in Ontario 1920s to 1950s. p.123.

When Great Britain and her allies France and Russia went to war against Germany and Austria, in August 1914, Canada became involved. Although Confederation had made Canada a separate country in 1867, Canada was still part of the British Empire. When Britain declared war on Germany, Canada was at war automatically. At the beginning of the war Canada had a very small voluntary force, however, by the fall of 1914, thirty-three thousand Canadian soldiers landed in Britain for training.

City of Toronto Archives,
Fonds 1244, Item 2439

These men, who had been the core of the work force, left it at exactly the time when increased productivity became essential in order to sustain life at home and supply the war effort. This absence of men and the tremendously increasing demand for workers created both new stresses and unprecedented opportunities for women at home and abroad. The organizing skills they had learned would equip them to face the challenges ahead.

GREEN DRAGON PRESS

Part 1:
On the Home Front

The Shell Finisher by Frances Loring (1888-1968), bronze. Frances Loring and her companion, Florence Wyle, received commissions from the War Records Office during World War I. Much of their work from that period shows women engaged in industrial war work.
Canadian War Museum, National Museum of Civilization, 84-8340.

Women were the subject matter of propaganda posters aimed at encouraging men to enlist, and were also encouraged to contribute to the war effort in a wide variety of ways.

Right: Patent medicine advertisement called on women to help win the war, stressing the value of "Dr. Pierce's Favourite Prescription" to make them strong and healthy.
Courtesy Moira Armour

WOMEN ARE NEEDED

TO

HELP WIN THE WAR

WOMEN CAN be usefully employed in nursing the wounded, in making up the soldiers' kits and a thousand other ways—BUT

THEY MUST BE STRONG and HEALTHY

DR. PIERCE'S FAVORITE PRESCRIPTION MAKES WEAK WOMEN STRONG.

It can now be had in Tablet form at all Druggists.

fight for her

COME WITH THE IRISH CANADIAN RANGERS OVERSEAS BATTALION MONTREAL

Lt.Col. H.J.TRIHEY - O.C.

Left: Whistler's Mother Propaganda poster.
Hal Ross Perrigard, Lithographer, after Whistler.
Poster, 87 x 55 cm. Harris Lithographing Co. Ltd.
Toronto, ca 1917.
Library and Archives Canada/First World War Collection/Acc. No. 1983-28-1017/C-095738.

Introduction

World War I demanded the participation of a large number of Canadian men. This opened up many opportunities for women that were previously closed to them. Women were an essential component of the Canadian war effort and their efforts on the home front, in the factories, as well as on the battlefront were important to a successful outcome.

Thousands of women were employed by the military, working at a variety of jobs such as motor transport work. Many went overseas as ambulance drivers; worked in supply depots and as trained nurses and nursing aids. A total of 3,141 women enlisted as nursing sisters in the Canadian Army Medical Corps Force. Forty-six died during the war from drowning, disease and air raids that struck field hospitals. A number of wealthy women organized relief efforts in Belgium and France. Most Canadian women did support the war; a few did not. Some of the women who did object worked in the Peace movement.

As the propaganda mills swung into action, appealing to women to "send their men to war," and to take up their tasks at home, women volunteers organized hospitals, nursing homes and canteens. They rolled bandages and helped tend to the wounded. Thousands of other women worked in Canadian weapons factories. Between 5,000 and 6,000 women were employed in the civil service and many others worked in offices and on farms. Women also organized charitable associations and sent food and supplies to the soldiers overseas. Thousands of socks and blankets were sent overseas to battlefronts.

There was even a brief flirtation with civil defence, though the idea of women armed with rifles was too much for the authorities and that effort was soon squelched.

Mass media, in the form of large newspapers, glossy magazines and widespread radio communication, was an invention of the twentieth century. It made it possible to spread systematic advertising of the point of view of those in power in an entirely new way. A huge propaganda campaign, of a scope and influence never before possible, began early in World War I. Its aim was to pressure, even guilt, men into fighting and women into serving to support the war.

GREEN DRAGON PRESS

an Instrumental Solo. A Paper was read by Mrs Duke. Cereals and their value as breakfast foods. All sang Tipperary then a Reading by Mrs George Rawn "Waterloo". Roll was called and members gave the place of their birth. Meeting closed with singing of the National Anthem.

Jan 28.

A Special meeting was held at Mrs. Ira Stoiks to pack a bale for the Red Cross Society. The following articles were sent;

1 pair pillows & 1 pair Socks. Mrs Haffey.
1 " pillows & 1 pair pillow cases. Mrs Lemon
1 " pillows & 1 pair " cases Mrs. D. N Potter
1 " pillows 2 " pillow cases.
8 handkerchiefs 1 chest Protector. Mrs. Jas. Armstrong
1 day Shirt. Mrs. Wesley Kee.
1 pair of pillows, 1 pair pillow cases
1 night dress, & 10 bandages. Mrs. T. Mason.
2 pair socks. Miss Lizzie Mills
1 " Socks & 1 night dress. Mrs. W. Atkinson
2 " Socks. Mrs Alex Jackson
1 " Socks & 1 night shirt. Mrs. Wm Leggett
1 " Socks & bandages. Mrs Lewis
2 " Socks. Mrs. Jas Taylor
1 " Socks. Mrs. Wilson Duke
1 " Socks. Mrs. Do. Potter
1 " Socks. 1 Shirt. Mrs. A. R Mills

Minutes of the meeting.
Dufferin County Museum and Archives, Rosemont, ON.

GREEN DRAGON PRESS

Propaganda

Notices published in newspapers urged women to pressure men to go to war, and posters used images of women to encourage men to enlist.

Advertisements for specific products urged women to stay strong and healthy to help with the war effort and to buy certain products to make sure they did.

Many of these notices and advertisements used military language in their efforts to make women feel part of the war. Thus, once the women "enlisted" and were "serving on the home front," they were urged to make specific contributions. These requests included tobacco. This may seem odd to us now but clearly it was considered essential for the men fighting in the trenches.

One such contribution was to send supplemental supplies to the soldiers. Before the war had gone on for long, every woman in Canada was either related to or knew men at the front, and women's organizations, both established and new, responded enthusiastically to the challenge.

Women's groups met regularly to pack Red Cross parcels. The *Labour Gazette* reported in July 1915 "The efforts of the various women's organizations of the city have been for the last months in the direction of patriotic work. During the month of June twelve tons of linen was collected by the Daughters of the Empire and forwarded to the headquarters of the Red Cross Society in England, while socks to the number of 1,800 pairs were collected on Empire Day and

sent to England to be distributed among the soldiers." And in Dufferin County, Ontario women met to hear musical entertainment, a paper about cereals and their value as breakfast foods, and a reading of "Waterloo." They sang "It's a Long, Long Way to Tipperary" as they sorted and recorded the articles made by the group to be sent to England. A roll call was held, each woman giving her place of birth, and the meeting ended with the singing of *God Save the King*. As the war neared its end, Black women formed the Women's Charitable Benevolent Association to look after the poor and sick, to run soup kitchens and to provide temporary homes for returning soldiers.

Grand Valley, World War I Red Cross Women's Institute Autograph Quilt. 1916.
From the quilt collection of Dufferin County Museum and Archives, Rosemont, ON.
(A99-303-1-1).

The Story of the Autograph Quilt

Dufferin Museum description: Red & white cotton quilt (no batting) 87" x 72" -approximately thirty 11" white blocks with names embroidered in red; cotton floss, sashed and bordered in 3" wide strips of red cotton; back is twill woven cotton bordered in red cotton; quilting is inside the blocks & diagonally through the blocks.

Each name on the quilt represents a donation of ten cents, which went to the Grand Valley Red Cross society to be spent eventually on supplies and comforts for the soldiers from the village. Donors wrote their names on the squares, the women embroidered the names and then the quilt was assembled and displayed in its finished state. The money collected was used to buy supplies - wool to knit sweaters, and treats and medicines for the soldiers. While the society was trying to decide where to send it to do the most good, a call came for bedding from the front-line hospitals in Europe. So it was enclosed in a shipment to France. Nothing more was heard of it for several years. Then one day, quite a while after the end of the war, a citizen whose name appeared on the quilt, was amazed to receive a parcel from France, which contained a dirty old quilt, stiff and stained. It was the autograph quilt. It was accompanied by a letter, which told of its being found in an Allied trench after the end of hostilities, by a Frenchman, who realizing the possible value it might have as a souvenir of the war, took it home. Then one day he thought perhaps the quilt should be sent back to Canada to a name and place on the quilt. So back across the sea it came. It was washed as clean as possible, and hung in the entrance of the then new Carnegie library. A local resident remembered that the colours were a vivid red and a pure white except where a stain remained to tell of the heroism of some brave man. Faded from years hanging on the library lobby wall, in her mind it was still as beautiful as ever. When the library was being redecorated, it was decided to take down the quilt and burn it, along with old books and papers. Birdie Boswell's father, William George Boswell rescued the quilt and took it home; later he gave it to his daughter. She kept the quilt safe for several decades and then when the Dufferin Museum was built, the Autograph Quilt found a new home.

Dufferin County Museum and Archives, Rosemont, ON.

Not only did women gather food and clothing for the war effort, they had to raise funds to send the goods because there was no discount in postage to send these things overseas. The following article in a local newspaper reported on the federal government's response to requests for free or reduced postage.

Dufferin County Museum and Archives, Rosemont, ON.

PARCELS FOR THE BOYS

Postage Must be Paid—Canada Cannot "Deadheadf"

Ottawa, Nov. 30.—The Post Office department is in receipt of applications to have parcels addressed to soldiers in France sent free or at reduced rates of postage, there evidently being an impression that the department has control of these rates and could do as it wished. This is not so, as the question of postage is fixed by international agreement. Under international law, provision is made for the free transmission of parcels for prisoners af war, but this privilege does not extend to parcels for troops engaged in active service, nor is it within the power of the department to so extend it.

If the addressee is England, the rate on parcels fo England applies, which is twelve cents pound; whilst if he is in France the parcels are subject to the rates applicable to parcels for France, which are : 1lb., 32c; 2 lbs., 40c; 3 lbs., 48c; 4 lbs., 64c; 5 lbs., 72c; 6 lbs., 80c; 7 lbs., 88c; 8 lbs., $1.02; 9 lbs., $1.10; 10 lbs, $1.18; 11 lbs., $1.26.

These are exactly the same charges which existed for years before the war. In all cases. parcels for the troops must be addressed care of the Army Post Office, London, England.

"Ottawa, Nov. 30. — The Post Office department is in receipt of applications to have parcels addressed to soldiers in France sent free or at reduced rates of postage, there evidently being an impression that the department has control of these rates and could do as it wished. This is not so, as the question of postage is fixed by international agreement. Under international law, provision is made for the free transmission of parcels for prisoners of war, but this privilege does not extend to parcels for troops engaged in active service, nor it is within the power of the department to so extend it."

Dufferin County Museum and Archives, Rosemont, ON

Women's organizational skills provided the basis for their expanded work, both volunteer and paid, in support of the war effort. Established organizations expanded or changed their focus, and new groups sprang up.

Middle-class and well-to-do women formed knitting and sewing clubs. Knitting even became acceptable in church. Women made garments for men stationed overseas, rolled bandages and raised money for hospitals and canteens on the front.

Women hold bazaar for war aid.

In Vancouver, women of the Garvey Movement organized a branch of the Universal Black Cross Nurses, and Negro societies in Toronto, Montreal, and Halifax solicited funds and distributed propaganda leaflets, occasionally in cooperation with larger white fraternal organizations. (Robin Winks, *The Blacks in Canada*; p. 319) At least one Black woman trained as a nurse in New York, and is believed to be the first Black nurse to practice in Canada during WWI, though not overseas. While Black women were excluded from most of the better-paying jobs in munitions factories, they did find ways to help the war effort, and it was a Black woman, Hattie Rhue-Hatchett, from North Buxton, Ontario, who wrote the song "The Sacred Spot," which the soldiers adopted as a marching song.

Buxton National Historic Site & Museum.

During World War I, Canadians believed that a German invasion was a real possibility. As a nation within the British Empire, Canada felt as vulnerable to invasion as Britain itself. So on the one hand, for women to take up arms came as a real shock. On the other hand, by forming paramilitary organizations and learning to shoot, they were simply preparing to defend their country should the worst happen and enemy troops land in Canada.

Between 1914 and 1916, women's home guards became active in Winnipeg, Edmonton, Montreal and Toronto. Jessica McNab, founder of the Toronto Home Guard, pointed out that trained and armed women would free more men for

Women Learn to Shoot
City of Toronto
Archives,
Fonds 1244,
Item 981

"overseas duties. At the very least....military drill and discipline," McNab contended, would produce "a body of women whose muscles and nerves are under perfect control [who] would be a tower of strength in an emergency."

In many parts of Canada, women enrolled in civil defense courses to protect their homes against invaders and saboteurs. A group of Toronto women, pictured here, learn to fire rifles in 1915. The group was organized by Jessie McNab. Lt. Col. J. Galloway supervised training.

Both Patriots and Proper Ladies: Canadian Women's Paramilitary Participation, 1860 – 1920

Korrie Street

It began inauspiciously: a small notice appeared at the end of an announcement regarding the availability of first aid classes and examinations. It read simply that "recruiting would take place for a women's home guard that evening at Dundurn Heights, 850 St. Clair Avenue West." (1) No one reading the newspaper on August 17th, 1915 could have predicted that the organization, which became known as the Toronto Women's Home Guard and later the Canadian Women's Home Guard, would ignite the energies of 1,000 Toronto women and capture the imagination of the entire city. What some commentators regarded as a joke turned out to be a vibrant and popular, albeit brief, women's paramilitary movement in wartime Toronto.

The Women's Home Guard and other women's paramilitary organizations have been virtually ignored in traditional histories of Canada's participation in the First World War. Usually they are dismissed as aberrations or discussed as quaint anecdotes to lighten the more serious history. Women who chose to participate in movements such as the Home Guard instead of the Red Cross or the Imperial Order Daughters of the Empire (IODE) are portrayed as overly enthusiastic or misguided. They are neither.

When war broke out in Europe in August 1914, few in Canada were prepared for the profound impact that it would have on Canadian society. By the war's end, one out of every ten men

of the Canadian Expeditionary Force (CEP) had been killed and at least twice that number had been maimed or disabled. But the First World War also left its mark on those who did not serve on the battlefield. As young men volunteered for military service, women rushed to join the war effort in other capacities. Women were as enthusiastic as men about the prospect of war. Women war workers, patriotic clubwomen and nurses may be the images we are most familiar with, but there were other women who desired to serve Canada in a military capacity.

To begin with, any assumptions that we may have regarding women's unfamiliarity with the trappings of the military should be dispelled. By trappings, I refer to the drill, uniforms, customs and weapons of military forces. Drilling for women appears to have been quite common in the late nineteenth century. For example, women were involved with the drill teams of the Red Cross and the St. John's Ambulance Corps. (2) Their uniforms were military in style and they were often pictured with rifles or pikes. Two groups in particular demonstrate that the existence of such women's paramilitary groups was popular and acceptable in pre-WWI Ontario society.

The first group was known as Lady Stanley's Cadets. These St. Catharines "girls," named in honour of the wife of then Governor General Lord Stanley were uniformed in military style and were armed with the Snider rifle, the same rifle that was issued to army

GREEN DRAGON PRESS

regulars in the 1860's. The actual purpose of the unit is unknown, but they were popular at many events. Most notably, the women performed a benefit in aid of St. Mary's Roman Catholic Church on March 21, 1892. The cadets were commanded by Captain George Thairs, from the 19th Lincoln Regiment, who was a Master at Ridley College, and Lieutenant John Campbell, who later became a judge. I would argue that a group which is commanded by a Master at a respected college and is asked to perform at a benefit for the Church could not have been unacceptable, unconventional or abnormal. (3)

Another group of cadets which suggests the popularity of women's paramilitary activities before WWI was the London Girls Cadet Corps. Like the St. Catharines group, they dressed in military uniform, carried rifles and practiced military drill. The girls were described as the "debutantes of the period, Collegiate girls, [and] daughters of London's best-known families." One of its former members described the purpose of the Corps as for, "the sake of healthy drill and the desire to promote a spirit of loyal and patriotic comradeship..." the young women learned how to handle a rifle and how to shoot straight." (4) Again I would suggest that inclusion of the daughters of the best London families precludes too many assumptions of abnormality.

It should not surprise us either that women chose to support the war by joining home guards or that the Toronto Women's Home Guard was not the only women's unit that was active during the war. On July 22, 1915, *Saturday Night Magazine* reported that women in Winnipeg,

Manitoba, had taken up arms. (5) One week later, *Saturday Night* ran an article revealing that women in Edmonton had formed a Women's Reserve Corps and the next week's edition brought yet another report of women's paramilitary activities. The patriotic women in Montreal had formed the Women's Volunteer Reserve. Like the Home Guard, they practiced riflery and drill. (6) In April 1916 *Maclean's* Magazine reported that women's home guards were active in Toronto, Vancouver, Montreal and Winnipeg.

The goal of such units was to assume the responsibilities of home defence in order to release men for overseas duty. Jessica McNab founded the Toronto Home Guard to ensure that women were as prepared as possible for aiding the war effort in any and every way possible. She believed that women could indeed be trained as soldiers. Ideally, she had hoped that they would assume the duties of the home defence units thereby releasing men for overseas duties. At the very least, she believed the female recruits could become self-sufficient enough not to require an inordinate amount of protection or assistance from men. Military drill and discipline, McNab contended, would produce "a body of women whose muscles and nerves are under perfect control [who] would be a tower of strength in an emergency." (7) When asked in August of 1915 if they really meant to fight or engage in battle, the Commander of the Guard replied with an emphatic "Yes, if necessary for home defence." Speaking of her recruits, she added that, "they are ready to do anything that a woman can do. We are opening a rifle range next Saturday." (8) Laura E. McCully, one of the notorious guardswomen and the treasurer of the unit, believed that training women in military discipline would make Canada impregnable. She argued that:

A Country in which all the young women are a reserve force cannot be invaded.
There would be nobody on whom the invaders could lean for support.
All the population would be in active service. (9)

Women who joined paramilitary units during the First World War believed that they were contributing to the war effort, and they were. They deserve to be included in historical accounts of Canada in the Great War.

1. *The Toronto World*, 17 August 1915, p. 4.
2. City of Toronto Archives, Williams James Collection, p. 706.
3. For information regarding Lady Stanley's Cadets, see *The Daily Standard*, 18 March 1892, p. 4, 22 March 1892; Craig Swayze, "Glimpses into our Past," No. 117 in *The Standard*, 21 January 1894.
4. "London Debutantes Formed Smart Cadet Corps While Boer War Enthusiasm High," *London Free Press*, 12 March 1936.
5. *Saturday Night*, 22 July 1915.
6. See Saturday Night, 2 July 1915, p. 22; 31 July 1915, p. 27; 7 August 1915, p. 25.
7. "Women Are Taking Soldiers' Training," *The Toronto World*, 25 August 1914, p. 4.
8. "Women's Home Guard Will Wear Khaki," *The Globe*, 26 August 1915, p. 6.
9. "Women's Home Guard Open City Hall Tent," *The Toronto Daily Star*, 27 August 1915, p. 4.

GREEN DRAGON PRESS

Women on the Farm

Many farm workers enlisted in the army, and if Canada was going to produce enough food, labourers had to be found. Farm work, promoted as a paying job, in fact became a drain on the financial resources of many women. Pay was usually $4 a week. In many places, room and board were provided, but in the Niagara area the women had to pay for both and were required also to help with food preparation and clean up and to keep the grounds where they lived in tents, clean and maintained. When rain or lack of crops depleted the work, a woman could pay more for her keep than she earned in a week. Erskine Keys's complaints echoed from Prince Edward Island to the prairies. And just as she eventually came to like the work, others who stuck with it long enough came to enjoy living on the land and farming.

The need to send inexperienced women from the cities to work on farms arose because the demands of war had created a shortage of labour in many Ontario industries; agriculture was no exception. Farmers, desperate for workers, although skeptical of the plan, finally agreed to listen to a government scheme to use "city girls" to harvest small fruits and vegetables such as strawberries, apples, tomatoes and beans (Report of the Trades and Labour Branch for 1917, Vol I., Part IV, 1918, p.47).

Actually, it was not unusual for Ontario farmers to use working-class and Native girls and women during the harvest. However, the increased opportunities for such women to work in urban factories during the war and the overwhelming demand for food created by the war effort forced farmers to consider new sources of labour. Many middle-class women students did not work for pay during the summer months and these were seen as a potential new labour source.

At twenty-three, Erskine Keys had just graduated from the University of Toronto. She was one of many women from urban centers who went to Ontario's Niagara Peninsula during the summers of 1917 and 1918 to harvest fruit. While she was there, Keys wrote home almost every day. In her first week in the countryside she complained of the lack of work due to bad weather in this letter to her mother.

> I'd give anything to come home...this is not a paying job...only 3 _ hours work
> all week...It's too expensive to stay here doing nothing [never mind] the agony.
> I can't stand it...the fields are full of water.... I'll come home and work, at least there will be
> no board to pay....I told one man that I had left a perfectly good job in the city and he told
> me to go back to it.

(Before going to Beamsville, Keys worked at the T. Eaton Company and at the Maclean Publishing Company for $7.35 and $7.50 per week respectively.)

Excerpt from: "...this is not a paying job": the Farmerette Movement in Ontario during the Great War by Margaret Kechnie. Quoted with permission.

GREEN DRAGON PRESS

Teacher Winnifred Cassel and three friends working on the farm: In: *Speak With Their Own Voices: a documentary history of the Federation of Women Teachers' Associations of Ontario,* by Pat Staton and Beth Light. Photo courtesy Winnifred Cassel.

Denny House, Bramsville, Ont.
Sunday, July 1st. 17.

Dear darling wee Beadie,

Thanks ever so much for the letter I got yesterday. Lady, I was glad to get it. Poor wee Beadie, Teenie's so sorry her wee Beadie is lonely. I'd give simply anything to come home. Certainly this is not a paying job. Just fancy! Only 3½ hrs. work all week. I think if we don't get work before Tues. I'll come home. It's too expensive to live here doing nothing — to say nothing of the agony. I can't stand it. I simply must come home if we don't get work. Of course I don't think it's the farmers' fault — it's the weather. They say they've never had so much rain before. Half the fields are buried under water so I expect half the crops of fruit are ruined. Just this morning Spedes & I passed a field of green onions completely covered with water all except their tops. I wouldn't be a farmer for anything. And guess what! That fool Miss Harris has sent for the other 40 (forty!) girls to come up to-morrow. I call it a crime. Four girls in the bunch have had work for the last three days & made $3.20. Rita & I & Spedes & about six others are the only others who have made anything. So I think I might as well come home & get a job in the city — where at least I don't have to pay my board. I'm sure we won't get any work to-morrow because it's pelting rain now & the farmers don't seem to need us either until August & they don't say anything when we say we wonder if 75 girls will get work. So what's the use of staying this month. This weather is proving fatal to the fruit. Last year they needed workers awfully badly, but I don't see that they'll need us this year. I think it would pay to come home until they find out for sure that they need us. Don't you think so? Please tell me in your next letter darleen, what you really think, & if we don't have work before then, I'll come home. One man whom I told I'd left a perfectly good job in the city to come here, advised me to go back so I think I will

An Opposite View

Francis Beynon was one feminist who was certainly not a "wholehearted, uncritical patriot." The daughter of Methodist farmers who moved from Ontario to southwestern Manitoba and then to Winnipeg, the strong-minded and eloquent young woman saw Winnipeg as a place to found a new social order. She wanted to make Christianity relevant to the modern world, but was wary of the notion of a socialist utopia. She was hired as women's editor of the *Grain Growers Guide*. At first she was popular, though her columns dealt more with women's rights and pacifism than household questions. With the onset of the war, Beynon assumed that feminists would lead the fight to end the war. This, and her commitment to the immigrants in the north end of Winnipeg, set her against Nellie McClung and the majority of women in the suffrage movement, most of whom were upper class and British in origin, and many of whom had sons in the trenches (as did McClung). McClung actually argued that only women born in Canada or Britain should be given the vote and in fact she would urge women to use their vote to support conscription.

Prior to the war, prejudice against foreign born people certainly existed, but the war provided an excuse to openly express distrust of people who had come from countries Canada was fighting. Beynon continued her outspoken opposition to the war and was finally forced out of her job at the paper and moved to New York in 1917 to join her sister and brother-in-law, the journalist Vernon Thomas, who had himself been fired from the *Winnipeg Free Press* for publicly supporting left-wing MPP F.J. Dixon's antiwar speech in the provincial legislature. In her farewell column, Francis explained that she was going to "that Mecca for all writers…the city of New York." She later published a novel, *Aleta Dey*. The heroine was a Winnipeg farm journalist, feminist, and Christian pacifist, and many viewed the book as non-fiction. Beynon worked at a mission and wrote a few articles for American reform journals but little else is known about her years in New York. She returned only once to Winnipeg just before her death in 1951.

GREEN DRAGON PRESS

"We'll allot you the first set of the howitzer shells"

The foreman met me at the door, and he just beckoned to me. The reason why he couldn't say anything was because you couldn't have heard him! And I just had to follow him. I went through all these avenues and avenues of clanking, grinding, crashing machines. Some of them were so close together that in order to get to their machines they'd built a kind of a stile – several steps up, and then you walked across, and then you went down again….Well the foreman led me in behind this machine, and I stood by the wall and watched. He demonstrated how to do one shell, and then he pointed to me. And so I very gingerly walked up to the machine and did what he had done. Then he stood there and said, 'Again!' and I did another one. Then he just waved me goodbye and off he went. I was panic-stricken. But I got used to it, so used to it that pretty soon I was looking around me seeing what my fellow workers were like….

The shells came out of the blasting furnaces first, and then they would have to be put out into the yards to cool. And then gradually they were brought in and they were put on this conveyor belt. I was near the end with my back to the wall. Those things came along there, and there was a woman in front of me and on the side opposite to me, she did the first cut and I did the first cut. We pushed a lever and that lifted the shells up onto this conveyor belt and then a man—I don't know how he got there, I don't know what he did—but I just remember that he did something that lowered it into our machines. When the shell came, I pushed this lever and the belt caused a knife to go just against the shell, and then it would start to peel. The shell was turning all the time. I pushed that lever against it. It would turn, and you had to quickly knock off these jagged long pieces before they got as far as your face, because they would just swing around, back and forth. You just knocked them off, and they fell behind the machinery. I imagine that every once in a while they had to go and clear all the jagged stuff out. Then the next machine to me did the next cut and so on until it got to the end of the row. Then it was just like a beautiful piece of polished steel. Then it had to go some other place for other things. Oh yes, and right over there where this thing was—it looked like a great big chisel--was this little tap. Just before you put your machine on, you turned that little tap so it was pouring chemicals…that was what got all over us.

Elaine Nelson: *The Great War and Canadian Society: An Oral History,* ed. Daphne Read, p. 53.

GREEN DRAGON PRESS

New Opportunities for Employment

Perhaps the greatest change for women during World War I was the tremendous expansion of opportunities for employment. Of course women had always worked in the home and many widowed, single and/or poor women had worked, often in very poor conditions and almost always for far less pay then men doing comparable jobs. But many kinds of work we expect to see women doing were, before 1914, closed to any woman, however qualified, however able and eager to do the work. Women who had never been in paid employment and women who had been domestic servants, clerks or factory workers moved into better-paying jobs. More than 30,000 women went to work in munitions factories, between five and six thousand entered the civil service and many more worked in banks and offices.

Women Munitions Workers. Threading set screw holes - No. 80 BR, T.8.P Fuse, Russell Motor Car Co. Ltd., Toronto, Ont. ca 1917. Library and Archives Canada/Department of National Defence Collection/PA-024639.

Women in munitions factories worked between ten and sixteen hours a day and earned from twenty to forty-five cents per hour. As the war continued, other industries such as aircraft production and shipbuilding opened to women; however, female labour was widely viewed as a temporary phenomenon, a patriotic contribution to the war effort. When hostilities ended, so did many of the jobs. These new jobs had provided an independence the women had never experienced.

Even with all this need for workers, for the most part, the marketplace remained closed to Black women. While their voluntary contributions to the war were not turned down, and many of their men went off to do some of the worst jobs at the front, these women were not allowed to work in factories. Robin Winks states that this was the lowest point in their history for the Black community in Canada. There were about 20,000 African Canadians in Canada at the time. Why did the dominant society need to treat a small, and in many cases invisible, group of people so badly? As Sylvia Hamilton notes, during this period, "African Canadian women…were facing widespread discrimination and exclusion in all aspects of their lives not only because of gender. For them, race also sharply etched the parameters of their place in Canadian society." (see *Black Women in Canada: Past and Present*, Marguerite Alfred).

Little documentation exists concerning First Nations and Asian women in paid employment during this period. In the west coast fishing industry, white men, Native men and Asian men worked on descending wage scales. Asian men made more than white women, and white women made more than Native women, who made more than Asian women. It appears that this system changed little if any during the war. If this kind of division by race at all reflects general trends, First Nations and Asian women remained almost totally invisible, in dire poverty, and with little if any opportunity.

For many women who did have opportunities in the workforce, an entire new life opened up. In Kingston, Ontario, a woman walked into the office of the manager of the Kingston, Portsmouth and Cataraqui Electric Railway Company and requested a job as a conductor (she was called a "conductorette"). To ask an able-bodied man to do the job would keep him from active service, the job needed doing and she was able and eager. Since the manager could find no good reason to deny her the job, he hired her.

GREEN DRAGON PRESS

For one Black woman, though, the wartime shortage of teachers offered an opportunity.

Ada Kelly

Ada Kelly was the first Black woman hired to teach in the public school system in an Ontario School Board (Windsor, Ontario.) Her Normal School principal wrote her a glowing letter of recommendation, although to our contemporary eyes it seems patronizing and even racist. (see following pages)

In 1916, her salary for the year was $650. Inspectors' reports speak of her excellent teaching and organizational skills. In later life she was a strong community leader and served as a mentor and example to many younger members of her extended family.
Photo: courtesy Christine Kelly.

F. P. Gavin, B.A
Principal.

Windsor, Ont., Aug 17ᵗʰ 1913

W. J. Shrene Esq.
    Lec - Treas. Trustee Board,
     SS. U⁼ 4 Raleigh,

Dear Sir – I understand Miss Ada
Kelly (colored) of Windsor is an applica
for a position in your school. Permit me
to say a word on her behalf. I had
her in Windsor Coll. Just all through
her High School course and know
well her attainments and abilities.

    She was one of our best students
throughout her course and graduated
with an unusually broad and
thorough training. She is a young
woman of good ability, studious hab

and smith a very fine character.
If I could afford a private teacher
or governess for my own children
I know of no one whom I would
sooner have.

If you can give a colored
girl the position I feel sure you will
not regret trying Miss Kelly, if you should
do so. She is a much better teacher
than many a white girl. She is an
attractive looking young woman, well
mannered and always neatly dressed.

Yours truly,
F. P. Gavin

Windsor Collegiate, Windsor, Ont.   Aug. 17, 1913.
F. P. Gavin, B.A.
Principal.
1913

W. J. Shreve Esq.
Sec- Treas. Trustee Board
SS #4 Raleigh

Dear Sir

    I understand Miss Ada Kelly (coloured) of Windsor is an applicant for a position in your school. Permit me to say a word on her behalf. I had her in Windsor Collegiate Institute all through her High School course and know well her attainments and abilities.

    She was one of our best students throughout her course and graduated with an unusually broad and thorough training. She is a young woman of good ability, studious habits and with a very fine character. If I could afford a private teacher or governess for my own children I know of no one whom I would sooner have.

    If you can give a coloured girl the position I feel sure you will not regret trying Miss Kelly if you should do so. She is a much better teacher than many a white girl. She is an attractive looking young woman, well mannered and always neatly dressed.

Yours truly

F. P. Gavin

Courtesy
Christine Kelly

On Their Own

For the women at home who had husbands, sons and brothers fighting in Europe, the stress was unimaginable. Many of those they loved would never return and all too many who did survive were damaged physically and often mentally and emotionally as a result of the horrors of the war.

Waiting for letters, dreading the telegrams that could bring terrible news, they carried on as best they could, doing paid or volunteer war work, managing their husbands' businesses, raising children alone and trying to keep hope alive. Many soldiers' wives and families faced destitution because during the first months of the war, soldiers were not required to sign over portions of their pay to support their families at home, although some companies chose to continue to pay employees who enlisted. Even with the implementation of separation allowances, until the establishment of the Canadian Patriotic Fund there were many cases of poverty.

Grace Morris's brother Basil was the youngest officer in the No. 1 Canadian Tunneling Company, fighting underground, driving mineshafts deep below the earth of no man's land; later, as an observer in the Royal Flying Corps, he flew above the enemy lines amidst the bursting shells. Her older brother Ramsey, a lieutenant in the 38th Battalion, led his men over the top of the trenches in the face of enemy fire. At home, Grace knitted socks and scarves and packed boxes to be sent overseas. She worked in the canteen at Camp Petawawa and led the soldiers in the popular songs of the day. In November of 1916 Grace crossed the Atlantic to spend time with her brothers while they were on leave in England. In her ninetieth year, Grace produced her first book, which she began to write in order to tell her grandchildren about the Great War. She included dozens of letters received from the battlefield. At the beginning, Basil's letters to his sister were positive and cheerful but as a time wore on, although he attempted to remain positive it was clear that stress had begun to affect him greatly.
This is an excerpt from his last letter:

Belgium, March 15, 1917

…I haven't had any Canadian letters for ages and ages and am getting quite fed up on it. There are no Canadian letters coming into camp at all and it is rotten. I certainly want to hear how the world is going around and if you are still the same as usual. Letters are about our only things to look forward to and I miss them very much indeed…I hope Mother has not got nervous over me at all, and you might convince her that there is no more need to worry now than when I was in the trenches. Of course I happen to be at war, and these are dangerous times but no more now than in the Tunnellers, the only difference being that instead of running the risk of going up, I run the risk of going down. I never realized I could get so calloused about fellows going west as I am and it is the same for everyone. Vernon Castle has been very badly injured here. He got a direct hit by an anti-aircraft shell, but managed to land somehow which is very extraordinary, but nevertheless is pretty badly smashed up. It isn't a very nice sight seeing a man brought down, but I mustn't mention those things, must I, because they worry you people much more than they do me. We are all fatalists here and don't worry in the least. It is the only way, otherwise life would be miserable.

This letter I am afraid is rather dull and I hope it hasn't bored you to death.
Love Basil.

At noon on March 17, 1917, the plane carrying Basil and his pilot was shot down over Belgium.

GREEN DRAGON PRESS

Grace writes:

"The dreaded telegram beginning 'Regret to inform' reached Basil's home on the 19th of March. To my parents and me, it seemed at first unbelievable, but we had to accept the appalling fact that Basil was dead. The tragic news reached Ramsey in the trenches where he was serving with his battalion."

The family did not recover easily from the shock of Basil's death; they had closed their minds to the possibility of death, and in spite of the long casualty lists that appeared day after day, believed their loved ones led charmed lives. They felt they had to cling to this belief in order to carry on their daily lives. Within a few weeks they had to face the possibility of further tragedy with the news that Ramsey's regiment was taking part in the assault on Vimy Ridge.

"In the early hours of April 9, Easter Monday, backed by sleet and snow and a driving wind, fifteen thousand Canadians advanced in the first wave behind a steady artillery barrage towards the German positions on the ridge; a second and a third wave of infantry followed. In this battle the Canadian Corps wrested from the enemy one of the most formidable defensive positions on the Western Front. It was a great victory, but the casualties were severe. It seemed too much to endure until we learned that Ramsey had survived."

But This Is Our War, Grace Morris Craig.

Matilda Casselman Ness put every effort into keeping hope alive. She would not accept the fact that her son Garnet was missing, and went to great lengths to search for him. Her granddaughter Geraldine Morriss wrote about Matilda's quest.

"She [Matilda] enlisted in the Winnipeg Women's Volunteer Reserve intending to make her way to Europe as a member of the Reserve and, once there, to find her son. (I have sometimes mused that it was her own experience as a civil servant that resulted in her distrust of officialdom. The only thing she knew for sure was that Garnet was missing and that his body had not been found. The instant communication of today did not exist.)

Though she failed in her mission to travel to Europe, she hired aircraft to drop over Belgium and France leaflets bearing her son's photograph with names and addresses to contact in Kirkfield Park [no word was ever received].....

I decided as an adult that it would be useful to try and obtain some information about Garnet and how he died. I contacted the Commonwealth War Graves Commission in 1985, long after Matilda's death. Commission records show that Garnet went missing between April 22 and April 24, 1915 after a German poison gas attack and that there is no known grave. Whether or not grandmother came to accept Garnet's death is not known....

GREEN DRAGON PRESS

Matilda Ness died on Saturday, February 27, 1932 in Winnipeg at sixty-six years of age….Much later, I learned why we mortals cling to hope when there appears to be none. My much-loved and much-admired brother died when he was just twenty-eight and I clung to the hope until the day of his funeral that he would live, though we had been told he could not. Then, at last, I understood."

Geraldine Morriss, *Extraordinary Ordinary Women*.

Not all women were left to make decisions on their own. Sometimes absent husbands and brothers retained the right to exercise their authority long distance. The Shanly family was one of those. Mrs. Shanly was a widow with two daughters and a son, Lieutenant Colonel C.N. "Bob" Shanly who was a paymaster in the Canadian Expeditionary Force. He was first posted in England and later sent to Rouen, France, where he worked during much of 1915 and part of 1916. A devoted brother, he wrote many letters to his sister, Frances ("Coo"), who lived in Toronto. She in turn tried to make his life easier by sending him homemade jam, boxes of apples, knitted scarves, socks, blankets and other items that were in short supply in England and France during the war. These were much appreciated by her brother and the other men with whom he worked.

Unfortunately, Lt. Col. Shanly, while he was not assigned to fight in the trenches, appeared to be the victim of overwork. He contracted bronchitis in April 1916, spent some time in the military hospital in Rouen, and was then sent to England to recover. He died there in the late spring or summer of 1916. The letters do not give the exact date or precise cause of his death, but in an age without antibiotics it is likely that he died from complications of bronchitis or from pneumonia. We can see the evidence of his deteriorating health from the handwriting in his letters. Though the letters have a brotherly tone, there is no doubt that he expects his views to prevail, whether it be about an "unfortunate" love affair or negotiations to purchase a neighbouring property.

There are a number of themes in the letters: events in the war, comments on news from Canada, news of friends and family in both Canada and England, comments on the work that women did, and business dealings in Toronto. Examples of some of these themes from his letters are given below:

Rouen, February 8, 1916:
"We were all very much startled to read of the destruction of the Parliament Buildings at Ottawa, and I suppose there is no doubt as to the origin of the fire. It is the biggest thing these vandals have pulled off yet in that line, and I have no doubt there is great glee in Berlin."

Rouen, February 28, 1916:
"We had a Zeppelin scare here one night a short time ago, just before the L.77 was caught a short distance from Paris and destroyed. All the lights went out and the bells rang out vigorously. However, the Zep thought better of it and turned back, so that we did not get a view at all."

GREEN DRAGON PRESS

Rouen, March 19, 1916:
"I am glad to hear that the affairs of the Club (Toronto Ladies' Club where Frances was the secretary) are in such a flourishing state, and that the personnel of the Committee is so representative of what it should be. This is all very satisfactory, but I hope that they are also behaving in a satisfactory way in regard to emoluments for the Secretary!"

Red Cross Hospital, Rouen, April 28, 1916 (Shanly has been concerned about the news of a sudden love affair that Julia, possibly another sister, or another relation, has had in Toronto. He had written to Frances that he hoped that Julia would break off this affair, and in this letter it appears that he has received news that she had done so):
"In your last letter received on the 23rd, you make some remarks on poor Julia's case, and it strikes me that the first thing to do is to get her away from his mother for a long time, and a good way to do this would be for her to take up some hospital work in England such as Margot, Juliet, and Isabel [British cousins] are at present doing – scrubbing the floors and washing dishes, etc. – and shake all this romantic yellow-back novel business out of her head. There are also young girls of about her age doing exactly the same thing in this hospital."

London, December 21, 1916 – Letter from Aunt Elinor Kennedy to Frances Shanly. This letter was written some time after Lt. Col. Shanly's death, and it shows that Margot and Juliet had left the hospital and found other positions:

"Juliet seldom gets home before 8 o'clock. She is now at the War Office working in the Intelligence Dept. Soon she will get pay when she is perfect in typewriting. She has learnt very quickly and gets on very well. Margot has got the post of Superintendent of 5 canteens for munitions workers at Woolwich. They are run by the 'Ladies' Legion'…Lady Londonderry is the head. She asked Margot to take the work. She [Margot] goes to Woolwich five days a week and gets home by six o'clock. That is shorter hours than she had at the hospital, and being so much more in the open is better for her health. She is a voluntary worker and gets no pay, and in these times, everyone would like pay."
However, in a letter of January 11, 1918 from Aunt Elinor Kennedy to Frances Shanly, we read that:

"Margot and Juliet are at work all day as usual. And since working for the War Office, they get paid. They are both secretaries now, Margot with Admiral Mark Kerr who is on the Air Board, and Juliet with Colonel Williams, Military Railways. They find the work most interesting. They are at it early and late so that we never have dinner until 8.30…Isabel is working at a Canadian Recreation Hut in Boulogne. I think it is a very good change for her. She was so very depressed; her letters now seem more cheerful."

Shanly also discussed a number of business dealings in his letters to his sister. One in particular concerned the purchase of a property adjacent to the Shanly home on Willcocks Street in Toronto. In 1915 Frances Shanly had informed him that Mrs. Cameron, the owner of the neighbouring property, had died.

GREEN DRAGON PRESS

This is his response:

Rouen, July 12, 1915:
"...I suppose the house would be for sale, and I have often thought that it would be a very advantageous thing for us to own both houses...You might discuss the matter with Dyce and get him to make inquiries without it being known from whom the enquiries are being made as to the probability of the home being for sale and the price...I wouldn't like to say how much I should be prepared to give for the house, but I suppose it's worth about $6,500. If necessary I could put up some money myself, but I should like to hear what the chances are first and what Dyce thinks about it."

Rouen, August 24, 1915:
"I note your remarks about the Cameron house and the state of disrepair, which it is likely to be in. This had also struck me, and on thinking over the matter, would only consider the purchase if it could be secured at 'bargain rates' – certainly not more than $5000. I daresay it would require an expenditure of $1000 to put it in anything like decent shape, as it would have to be painted and papered throughout, and a good deal done to the exterior. I would also advocate putting in another bath, that is, converting one of the rooms into another bathroom. However, you might continue enquiries entirely 'on the quiet' and ascertain just how matters stand. If it was a case of a real bargain for cash, I might be able to find the money, or a good part of it, requiring only a small loan to be raised on the two houses together. The question of the high rate of taxation in Toronto now must also be taken into consideration, and for that reason, they cannot expect to get anything like what the house might have sold for a few years ago."

Several other letters referred to the purchase of the house and the need to keep the Shanly name out of it because of a fear that the heir to the house would inflate the value if she was aware of the prospective purchaser's name.

Rouen, October 24, 1915:
"However, keep your eye on it, and don't let it go altogether by default."

Nothing more for five months, then:

Rouen, March 27, 1915:
"I note what you say about the Cameron house and altho' I recollect having said that I thought $5000 was all it was worth in its present condition, still if it can be bought for $5,500, I will furnish $3000 in cash on the spot, and assume the existing mortgage which I understand is $2,500. Get Fleury to make that offer which is as far as I would go at present. Of course, it would be just as well not to let 'the family' know that the offer really comes from us! My idea is that the downstairs rooms could be utilized by Oniy[?] for her dancing classes and also by Jane for her school, and the upstairs rooms could be very profitably rented as bachelor apartments. This, of course, would mean some expenditure for furniture and a certain amount of repairs, which would have to be a matter for future consideration. In the meantime it could no doubt be rented as it stands for $50 a month."

GREEN DRAGON PRESS

By May 1916, Lt. Col. Shanly was seriously ill in a London hospital.

Second London General Hospital, Chelsea, W.W., May 12, 1916:
"I am not well enough to go any further into the matter of No. 17 at present, but I hope I will be able to be up again sometime before long, and will then give the matter some attention."

His last letter concerning the purchase of the house was dated May 12, the same day as the above letter.

London, May 12, 1916:
"I wrote you a note today, which I gave to Aunt Elinor to post. I am not quite sure what my offer for house (letter of 27 March) was, and you do not confirm it in your letter. My recollection, however, is that I offered $3,500 in cash and assume present mortgage of $2,500. Is this correct? It is all I could go at present..."

Here the letters cease. The archival collection includes a number of cards of condolence received by Frances and her mother, as well as the draft of a letter thanking the senders for their kindness.

The Shanly Papers, Baldwin Room, Metropolitan Toronto Reference Library. Research: Joyce Scane.

Women had always worked long and hard in the home. By the late nineteenth century they had begun to take the skills needed to run a household and to adapt those skills to social projects in the community as a whole. They moved, in other words, from the private sphere to include the public sphere in their range of activities. Women were no longer content to leave the running of the world to men; they had knowledge based on their everyday life that was available to few men. They took that very knowledge into the world.

Poverty, education, health and eventually the vote as a way to influence public policy in these matters, became their targets. World War I provided the opportunity to further expand and strengthen their skills, to learn new skills and for many women, for the first time, to earn their own money. These crucial shifts changed women's place on the home front and they proved their courage and abilities on the field of war. The combined changes resulting from women's experience in the war years would alter Canadian society forever.

Women at Clark's Lumberyard, Edmonton, April 1918. Glenbow Archives/NC-6-3311.

Chapter 2:
The Fight for the Vote

Presentation of a petition from the Manitoba Political Equality League,
23 December, 1915. Front L to R: Dr. Mary Crawford, Mrs. Amelia
Burritt, Back L to R: Lillian Thomas, Mrs. Fred Dixon.
Archives of Manitoba/Events 173/5(N9907).

PETITION

To The Honourable Members of His Majesty's Government of the Province of Manitoba, and the Honourable Members of the Legislative Assembly of the said Province.

WHEREAS the following resolution forms part of the resolutions of the Liberal Party as defining the Policy of Government of the said Party in the Province of Manitoba, that is to say:—

"The Liberal Party believing that there are no just grounds for debarring women from the right to vote, will "enact a measure providing for equal suffrage upon it being established by petition that this is desired by adult women "to a number equivalent to fifteen per cent. of the votes cast at the preceding general election in this Province;"

AND WHEREAS the Liberal party are now the party in office in the said Province;

NOW THEREFORE the petition of the undersigned humbly sheweth:—

Your Petitioners are women over the age of twenty-one years and are resident in the Province of Manitoba.

Your Petitioners are desirous that a measure shall be enacted forthwith extending the franchise to women on equal terms with men.

WHEREFORE YOUR PETITIONERS PRAY that there shall be enacted by the Legislative Assembly at the Session in which this Petition is presented to His Majesty's said Government a measure extending the franchise to women on equal terms with men.

AND your Petitioners as in duty bound, will ever pray.

Signature of Petitioners	Residence	Occupation

One strategy used by the suffragists to bring their cause into the public eye, or to the attention of legislators was the petition. In 1915, two petitions were presented by the Manitoba Political Equality League to the newly elected Liberal government of Premier J.C. Norris. One petition contained 39,584 names; the second contained 4,250 names all collected by 94-year-old Amelia Burritt.
Archives of Manitoba/Events 173/3(N9905).

GREEN DRAGON PRESS

Introduction

"For too long we have believed it our duty to sit down and be resigned.
Now we know it is our duty to rise up and be indignant."
Nellie McClung.

The first federal election in Canada was held in August 1867 but women were not allowed to vote. Even if women had been able to meet the same requirements around citizenship, property, age and race as men, the laws of the provinces of Nova Scotia, New Brunswick, Quebec and Ontario had been amended earlier in the 19th century to specifically exclude women from voting. It would be fifty years before relatively privileged, mainly white women, gained the vote, and almost a century (1960) before all women citizens over the age of 18, regardless of racial origin, had the right to vote and hold office in Canada at all levels of government. Disenfranchisement made women feel like second-class citizens and for many women this became increasingly unacceptable. In the late eighteenth and early nineteenth centuries women reformers were successful in introducing social reforms such as changes in married women's property laws, temperance, changes to education and employment laws, but women still did not have the vote and the political power that went with it. Leaders of women's organizations knew they needed this power to further the reforms they were dedicated to achieving. They challenged their opponents (and there were many) wherever and whenever there was an opportunity.

Speaking in 1913 to the National Council of Women, Sonia Leathes put the challenge clearly:

"It is on this account that women today say to the governments of the world: you have usurped what used to be our authority, what used to be our responsibility. It is you who determine today the nature of the air we breathe, of the food which we eat, of the clothing which we wear. It is you who determine when, and how long, and what children are to be taught and what their future prospects as wage earners are to be. It is you who condone or stamp out the white slave traffic and the starvation wage. It is you who by granting or refusing pensions to the mothers of young children can preserve or destroy the fatherless home. It is you who consider what action shall be considered a crime and how the offender, man, woman or child shall be dealt with. It is you who decide whether cannons or torpedoes are to blow to pieces the bodies of the sons which we bore. And since all of these matters strike at the very heart strings of the mothers of all nations, we shall not rest until we have secured the power vested in the ballot; to give or withhold our consent, to encourage or forbid any policy or course of action which concerns the people, our children, everyone."

The Woman Suffrage Movement in Canada, Catherine L. Cleverdon, p. xiii.

Opposition came from a number of sources, including those who wrote letters to the editor in the newspapers. Often the letters sought to place women on a pedestal and suggest that politics was no place for a woman:

GREEN DRAGON PRESS

"Women who believe in woman suffrage seem to think that we men want to deprive them of their liberties; but we wish to do no such thing. All men who are worthy of the name of men, place woman upon a very high pedestal, to which no man in his sphere, could ever hope to attain: and we want her to remain there, where she can command our respect and esteem and use the powers that God has given her for the good of humanity....Why should she besmear herself with the rottenness of politics?"

Satirical Valentine post card.
Canadian Women's Movement Archives/Archives canadiennes du mouvement des femmes.

GREEN DRAGON PRESS

Opposition also came from governments of the day.

Premier Duff Roblin of Manitoba, Nellie McClung's long time opponent in the battle for suffrage made the following statement to a suffrage delegation in 1914.

"Does the franchise for women make the home better? My wife is bitterly opposed to woman suffrage. I have respect for my wife; more than that, I love her; I am not ashamed to say so. Will anyone say that she would be better as a wife and mother because she could go and talk on the streets about local or dominion politics? I disagree. The mother that is worthy of the name and of the good affection of a good man has a hundredfold more influence in molding and shaping public opinion round her dinner table than she would have in the marketplace, hurling her eloquent phrases to the multitude. It is in the home that her influence is exercised and felt."

Like Premier Roblin, opponents of female suffrage believed that women should devote themselves to their home and family and predicted disaster if women entered public life. In the catalogue for the Public Archives of Canada exhibit (*The Widening Sphere: Women in Canada 1870-1940*), Jeanne L'Esperance described this view of women's role and the strategy devised by women suffrage leaders to counteract it:

"Traditionally, woman's sphere was the home, and the commonly accepted role for the adult woman was that of wife, mother and homemaker. With monotonous regularity those who debated this question throughout the nineteen and early twentieth century came up with the same answer.

The family was the fundamental building block of society and woman was its center. Yet technological innovation and industrial growth were inevitably impinging upon the home in this period. Mass production removed certain household tasks from the home to the factory, while labour-saving devices and ready-made food and clothing meant that domestic tasks consumed less and less time. Although new theories on infant care made mothering a more time-consuming task than it had been, the falling birthrate and increased life expectancy meant that parenting was not a lifetime task. At the same time disquietude at social changes made critics see any attempt by women to lead an independent life as an attack upon the family, and therefore upon the stable basis of society. On the other hand women had to prepare their children for the trials of the contemporary world. How could they do this if they were weak, helpless and uninformed and confined within their narrow sphere, the home? The answer, which women thinkers formulated, was the concept of 'maternal feminism', or widening their influence by taking out into the world the very qualities which made them so valuable within the family. Women were traditionally the culture bearers who passed on to their children the values and ideals of their society."

Nellie McClung suggested, with her usual biting wit, that there were hidden reasons for opposing votes for women.

"This deep-rooted fear, that any change may bring personal inconvenience, lies at the root of much of the opposition to all reform. Men held to slavery for long years, condoning and justifying it, because

GREEN DRAGON PRESS

they were afraid that without slave labor life would not be comfortable. Certain men have opposed the advancement of women for the same reason; their hearts have been beset with the old black fear that, if women were allowed equal rights with men, some day some man would go home and find the dinner not ready, and the potatoes not even peeled! But not many give expression to this fear, as a reason for their opposition. They say they oppose the enfranchisement of women because they are too frail, weak and sweet to mingle in the hurly-burly of life; that women have far more influence now than if they could vote, and besides, God never intended them to vote, and it would break up the home, and make life a howling wilderness; the world would be full of neglected children (or none at all) and the homely joys of the fireside would vanish from the earth. I remember once hearing an eloquent speaker cry out in alarm, "If women ever get the vote, who will teach us to say our prayers?"

Surely his experience of the franchised class had been an unfortunate one when he could not believe that anyone could not vote and pray."

Nellie L. McClung. "Speaking of Women," *MacLean's* Magazine, May 1916.

GREEN DRAGON PRESS

World War I, far from putting suffrage on the back burner, brought it to the forefront, with suffragists and government both recognizing the power that their war work gave women.

Most, though not all, suffragists supported the war effort and even as they worked to support it, they continued to struggle for the vote. Women finally won the right to vote in provincial elections for the first time in 1916 in Manitoba, Alberta and Saskatchewan. British Columbia and Ontario followed in 1917, Nova Scotia in 1918, New Brunswick in 1919, Prince Edward Island in 1922. Women in Newfoundland, which would remain a Crown Colony until 1945 when it joined Canada, gained the provincial vote in 1925. The last province to allow women to vote was Quebec, where women voted for the first time in 1940.

Right to Vote in Provincial Elections

Province	Right to Vote Provincially	Right to Stand for Provincial Office
Manitoba	January 28, 1916	January 28, 1916
Saskatchewan	March 14, 1916	March 14, 1916
Alberta	April 19, 1916	April 19, 1916
British Columbia	April 5, 1917	April 5, 1917
Ontario	April 12, 1917	April 24, 1919
Nova Scotia	April 26, 1918	April 26, 1918
New Brunswick	April 17, 1919	March 9, 1934
Prince Edward Island	May 3, 1922	May 3, 1922
Newfoundland	April 13, 1925	April 13, 1925
Quebec	April 25, 1940	April 25, 1940

GREEN DRAGON PRESS

At the federal level, most women, provided they were British subjects, obtained the right to vote in May 1918, shortly after the end of World War I. Aboriginal women obtained this right only in 1960. When women were finally granted the federal vote, it was as much due to the conviction of the Prime Minister, Sir Robert Borden, that they would support his party in the conscription crisis as it was to their acknowledged major contributions to the war effort.

So while many women were enfranchised, all conscientious objectors and naturalized British subjects who had been born in an enemy country lost their vote, and Dr. Augusta Stowe-Gullen, pioneer feminist, had the pleasure of observing anti-suffragists making speeches on the necessity and importance of women voting and even helping them get to the polls.

Most women of colour, including all Asian and Black women, did not get the vote until the late 1940s. Under the Indian Act, First Nations women were prohibited from voting for band councils until 1951. Only in 1960 did they get the vote in federal elections.

The Conscription Crisis

"One of the greatest crises in Canada during the war occurred in 1917. It centred around the issue of conscription. Conscription means that all able-bodied men would be required to join the army. Enlistment would no longer be on a voluntary basis…. Casualties were mounting daily on the Western Front. Military officials urged Borden to send even more Canadian troops to Europe. In Canada, volunteer enlistments were not keeping up with the number of men killed or wounded….The mention of conscription brought a storm of protest in some parts of Canada, especially among French Canadians. Many English Canadians believed that Quebec was not doing its part in the war….Why were there fewer volunteers from Quebec? The majority of Quebeckers were farmers, many with large families. Fewer farmers than city people joined the Armed Forces since farmers were considered essential to produce food for the war effort. But most French Canadians also did not share the enthusiasm that English Canadians felt for Britain's war. They did not believe that their sons should be forced to join the war. Many also did not feel any real tie to their country of origin, France. They felt they had been deserted by France when they were conquered by British forces in 1760. French language rights had been taken away in Manitoba and other western provinces, and in Ontario schools. French Canadians felt they were being treated like second-class citizens in Canada….The election of 1917 was particularly bitter. Conservatives and Liberals who believed in conscription formed a Union government. The split in Canada that Laurier had feared for so long had occurred. There were riots in Montreal and Quebec City against conscription. Four people were killed and many were injured. Troops had to be sent in with machine guns to restore order."

Spotlight on Canada, p. 118-119.

Conscription Crisis 1917: Sequence of Events

April 9
Heavy casualties during the Battle of Vimy Ridge.

May 18
Sir Robert Borden after his return from England decides that volunteers will not be enough to replace the losses and announces the intention to introduce conscription.

June 11
Borden introduces Military Service Bill into Parliament.

August 29
Military Voters Act passes Parliament. The vote was granted to all British subjects serving in the Canadian armed forces and provisions were made to conduct voting overseas.

September 14
The War Time Election Act becomes law. The vote is granted to all wives, sisters, mothers and daughters of soldiers who are serving or had served overseas. A large number of nurses were enfranchised by the act. The vote is denied to or taken from: those of enemy birth, those of European birth speaking the "enemy tongue" and conscientious objectors.

September 26
The Military Service Act becomes law. All males between 18 and 45 are eligible for compulsory military service. Exemptions are possible for conscientious objectors, persons working in essential war occupations, those doing work for which they had special qualifications and those for whom military service would cause special hardship.

October 12
A Union Government is formed from Conservatives and Liberals who left Laurier's Liberal Party.

November 25
The Union Government announces that sons engaged in production of food would be exempted from military service.

December 17
Election – The Union Government wins a landslide victory.

January
Conscription of men proceeds.

GREEN DRAGON PRESS

Women Exercise their Federal Franchise

Although the government provided financial support to the families of World War I soldiers, both by assigning part of servicemens' pay to their families and through the Canadian Patriotic Fund, they often found themselves in financial need. Mrs. R.D. Farquharson wrote to explain her circumstances in a letter to the Prime Minister, Robert Borden. As the wife of a soldier, Mrs. Farquharson had been granted the franchise. Her request for advice on how she should vote in the forthcoming December federal election was not very subtle.

Kamloops, B.C.
Nov. 27th, 1917.

Dear Sir---

I write to ask your opinion on which way a Soldier's wife with a family of seven should vote. As far back as I can remember we have upheld the Borden Gov. This year my husband is in France. When he enlisted (Feb. 1916) it was with the understanding that the C.P.F. [Canadian Patriotic Fund] were to make up what the Gov. lacked in providing as a living, since that time the price cost of living has gone up at least double and our allowance remains the same as it was when the C.P.F. was started. My oldest child is a girl eleven years old, my youngest 15 months, the price of fuel and clothing is awful as well as the price of the plainest foodstuffs. It is impossible to keep the family on $75.00 per month. I have asked the C.P. Society also the City for help and can't even get an investigation. I am ashamed to ask from the returned men who have done so much for us. Where there is being so much money wasted and spent on Election and such, surely it is not necessary that any little one's should suffer when a small cheque of perhaps 75.00 would meet extra expenses for winter and make us comfortable...

I remain yours;
To Win-the-War
Mrs. R.D. Farquharson
460 Columbia

Robert Laird Borden Papers, MG26 H, Vol. 61, 30683 Public Archives of Canada.

GREEN DRAGON PRESS

In her memoir of World War I, Grace Morris Craig recalled her part leading up to, and then in the election of December 17, 1917.

"By the end of 1917 the opportunity came for us to play our part on the home front. Great losses had been suffered by the Canadian expeditionary force at Vimy Ridge and other battles, and the casualties had to be replaced. One important province, Quebec, was not contributing its share and so conscription seemed inevitable. In the riding of North Renfrew my father had been chairman of the Conservative Association for a number of years; like most Canadians he realized that a coalition government would be necessary to bring in such a controversial measure. When the Union government was finally formed in October under Sir Robert Borden, a general election automatically followed; in North Renfrew a Liberal, Mr. Herbert Mackie, agreed to run for the new government.

For the first time, women would be allowed to vote, but they would be a very select group – the mothers, wives, and sisters of the men in the overseas forces. The job my father had chosen for me, which he had had in mind many months before when he begged me to return from England, was to organize the women voters of the riding. Upon my return I had taken a course in Isaac Pitman shorthand from a nun at the convent, and I asked several of my friends who had been in the business class there to help me form a committee. We were provided with a well-equipped office on Main Street in Pembroke. Through the nominal rolls of the overseas units we learned who the voters would be and we got in touch by mail with every one of them throughout the large riding.

There were no women's meetings called, but it was explained to all of them by letter that the only way they could hope to see their men again was to vote for the Union government and conscription.

On the night of the election, December 17, 1917, people crowded the armouries to hear the results, which came first by telephone in the riding and then by wire from the rest of Canada. The tension was great and angry looks were exchanged; but we had the great satisfaction of having helped to elect a coalition government that would bring in conscription, which we felt was our way of helping to win the war. We expressed our delight in loud cheering and scornful looks for the group of young men who did not like the results."

But This is Our War, Grace Morris Craig, p. 130.

GREEN DRAGON PRESS

Across the ocean, in Europe, nurses Ella Mae Bongard and Clare Gass recorded the date of the historic vote in their diaries:

December 9, 1917

"Voted tonight in the Canadian elections. A Canadian officer came out from Havre to arrange it. I feel quite important now. You may be sure I voted for conscription despite party politics for I don't want to see Canada drop out of the war at this stage."

Ella May Bongard in *Nobody Ever Wins a War*, ed. Eric Scott, p. 24.

Clare Gass was doubly qualified to vote. Under the Military Voters Act of August 1917, she qualified to vote as a member of the armed forces; under the Wartime Elections Act of September 1917 she qualified to vote as a female relative of an overseas soldier. The purpose of both these Acts was seen by many as a way to gain support for the Borden government, which by October 1917 had attracted a sufficient number of former opposition members from the Liberal Party to create a coalition Union Government. The election of this government in December 1917 gave the victory to Borden and his policy of conscription (compulsory military service). With her vote, Claire registered her support for a continuing supply of soldiers.

"Today about noon the Germans began to shell the Cross roads again one shell smashed the Estaminet at the corner into bits & several Belgians & soldiers were impaled there. Another shell burst just outside No. 3's Mess Hut. But fortunately no one was hurt. The sisters were all at lunch.

Hallie Carman just coming up to lunch was very near & thrown out on the ground. She is unhurt. I was asleep when the shelling began but the whir of the first shell overhead awakened me. The explosion shook the ground. I voted for the Union Government in Canada – this am."

The War Diaries of Clare Gass, 1915 - 1918, p. 184.

GREEN DRAGON PRESS

At home, a Toronto woman, Janie Smythe, whose sister was an army nurse, voted for the first time. The next day she wrote the following letter to suffragist Flora Denison, expressing her feelings about the experience of voting.

22 Glengrove Ave. W
Toronto Dec. 18, 1917

Toronto Dec. 18, 1917

My Dear Mrs. Denison.

It is befitting that you should be the first one I should write to since I recorded my first vote. It was a proud day yesterday for me and an hour, which you and others have by unceasing devotion to the cause, made possible. I may now be recognized by humanity at large, as having a complete number of organs and faculties with more or less average mental ability to use them! In a word am equal of my husband, at least technically speaking. I have my vote owing to my sister nursing soldiers. Stepmothers are not fully qualified for such a high honour as voting. I trust that when next we shall meet that I shall bear myself with true and becoming dignity in my new state of equality...

Janie Smythe

Mrs. Flora M. Denison Papers,
Thomas Fisher Rare Books,
University of Toronto Library
Mss Coll.

GREEN DRAGON PRESS

Liberal governments in Alberta and Saskatchewan hived military voters into separate constituencies. For this reason, the federal Conservatives designed the Military Voters' Act to allow soldiers to vote in their home ridings. In an election poster directed to soldiers and nurses from Alberta, they were reminded that under the Alberta Military Representation Act, they would have two votes and were exhorted to vote for nursing sister Roberta MacAdams.

Give One Vote to The Man of Your Choice
And the Other to the Sister

A picture of MacAdams appeared on the poster with the words; "She will work not only for your best interests but for those of your wives, mothers, sweethearts, sisters and children after the war."

When the Union Government was returned to power it recognized its debt to women by convening a Women's War Conference at Ottawa from February 28 to March 2, 1918. Delegates from all women's organizations in Canada were addressed by the Governor General and prominent Cabinet members on such topics as child welfare and national health. Finally, in March 1919, a bill was passed giving the vote to all Canadian women, though many women of colour and Aboriginal women were still excluded. Women voted for the first time in a federal election in 1921.

Nurses voting at No. 1 Canadian General Hospital, December 1917.
NA, PA 2279.

GREEN DRAGON PRESS

Chapter 3:
Far From Home

Nursing Sister Ruby Gordon Peterkin, 1916.
Library and Archives Canada/Acc. No. 1970-163/e002283118.

Edith Parkin

Edith Parkin, a former Chisholm, Ontario schoolteacher, nurse and World War I veteran is buried in Boxwell Cemetery. Parkin graduated as a nurse in 1913, worked in the United States until 1917, and then served in American Red Cross Hospital 25 in France. During her service, Parkin contracted hemolytic streptococcus and was discharged on September 19, 1919.

After a seven-year recovery period, Parkin became the nursing supervisor of a New York State hospital before returning to Chisholm Township to retire. When she died in 1955, her family could not afford a headstone to mark her grave. Her niece, Noreen Smith, regretted this for many years and in 2004 asked Chisholm Township Council to find the funds to put a marker on her aunt's grave.

Linda Thompson, a former councilor and genealogy enthusiast, took on the project. She enlisted the help of MP Anthony Rota, the Canadian Legion, the American Red Cross, and the U.S. military and U.S. war archives. Thompson was able to trace Parkin's Red Cross nurse's training and has her diary, which outlines her war experiences and the documentation of her nursing career. But Linda Thompson could not find Parkin's U.S. Army registration number and without that no financial support was forthcoming from either U.S. or Canadian military memorial funds. Edith had not registered for any pensions or benefits offered to those who served on active duty, probably because she was unaware of them. She is listed in the American Journal of Nursing's annual convention document as having been among those who served at Army Base Hospital 25. Thompson felt strongly that Parkin deserved to be recognized for her service. She called for donations and on July 23, 2005, in the Year of the Veteran, the marker was installed. Family, friends, politicians and Canadian and US military personnel attended the event.

Linda Thompson at the Edith Parkin headstone in the Boxwell Cemetery, Chisholm Township, prior to the unveiling.
Doug Mackay Photo.

GREEN DRAGON PRESS

Introduction

Many Canadian women were eager to serve overseas, and some opportunities were offered to them, mainly in medical units. Through persistence and ingenuity, women created other opportunities. Some women's desire to serve took them to France, Serbia, Africa and Belgium. And some, like a seventeen-year-old girl who dressed in boy's clothes, lied in an attempt to join the military.

To fully understand the wartime contributions of women far from home, we need to know their stories: who they were, why they volunteered, what their experiences were, and the impact of those experiences on their lives.

The largest group of women who served overseas was nurses, many of them volunteers. For the first time, nurses used their skills on a large scale to deal with the devastating results of modern battle – widespread injury from high-powered artillery, rapid-fire rifles, machine guns and, in this conflict, poisonous gas. These women paid their own way to Europe, bought their uniforms, worked long hours in dangerous, muddy, cold, rat-infested areas, and lived in flimsy tents in camps where there was less than enough to eat. Working to relieve suffering and to return as many injured soldiers as possible to combat, nurses contributed to the 89 per cent survival rate of Canadian soldiers who came under their care. Serving at casualty clearing stations just behind the front and at hospitals further back, nurses dressed and disinfected wounds, assisted at operations and helped patients' recovery by providing physical and emotional care when few vaccines were available and before antibiotics had been discovered. A total of 3,141 nursing sisters served in the Canadian Army Medical Corps in World War I: 2,504 in England, France and the Eastern Mediterranean at Gallipoli, Alexandria and Salonika. Forty-six of these women died and many more contracted various illnesses that involved months of recovery. Not only did nurses serve on the front, they risked their lives accompanying soldiers home on hospital ships. Fourteen nurses died in the sinking of the Llandovery Castle. Three were killed in the deliberate bombing of a hospital in France.

Not all the women of the Canadian Army's nursing service achieved their ambition of serving overseas. By the end of the war, there were 65 military hospitals in Canada employing 527 nurses. During the year 1918, for example, a total of 90,647 patients were treated in military hospitals in Canada. Those services would be needed in December 1917, when the disastrous explosion of a munitions ship in Halifax harbour killed 1,500 persons outright and wounded 5,000 others, 1,000 of them seriously. Surgeons and nurses from all parts of Canada and from the United States hurried to the scene to work under the direction of the Canadian Army Medical Corp.

Several Canadian women doctors served abroad. "If a woman wanted to serve overseas, then she either joined or formed a hospital unit, and these units then offered their services to the Red Cross or to one of the allied governments, and were sent wherever they were needed most" (*Those Indomitable Lady Doctors*, p.177). Among the Canadian doctors were Irma Le Vasseur from Quebec City, Ella Scarlett Synge of Vancouver, Mary Lee Edward and France Evelyn Windsor, both from Ontario.

GREEN DRAGON PRESS

Voluntary Aid Detachments (VADs), organized in Britain, trained thousands of nurses and orderlies to work in military hospitals. The VAD nurses were not very well trained and were assigned to act as assistants to the professional military nurses (also known as nursing sisters). They were usually given the most unpleasant tasks.

While most women served in medical capacities, some did other things, notably driving ambulances from the front to treatment areas near the front and then to hospitals. British war correspondent and later popular novelist and true crime writer Fryniwyd Tennyson Jesse, one of the few women journalists to go to the front, wrote about these women in British Vogue in 1918. "I received an impression of extraordinary beauty," she wrote. "The girls looked like splendid young airmen, their clear, bold faces coming out from between the leather flaps. They were not pretty, they were touched with something finer, some quality of radiance" (*Tapestry of War*, p. 444).

Thousands of women, usually the wives of officers, travelled to England to be near their husbands, often volunteering at canteens and other places where there was a need. Some, like Grace Morris, made the journey to be near a wounded relative.

When news reached the family that her brother Ramsey was in hospital at Manchester and threatened with blindness, it was agreed that Grace should go to him. Many "society" ladies devoted time to charities but were not terribly serious about their work. Mabel Adamson, however, was serious and used her organizational experience and contacts to create the Belgian Canal Boat project, carrying needed supplies to refugees in Belgium. Individual Canadian women, like Allie Douglas, who had special skills, found work in the War Office in London. Douglas was studying mathematics and physics at McGill University when the First World War erupted. She went to London to work in the War Office as a statistician. In 1918, at 23, she was awarded the Order of the British Empire for her work.

Patriotism, the wish to "do their bit," a chance for independence and, for some, adventure, motivated Canadian women to volunteer their skills. They did not question that Canada, as part of the British Empire, must participate in the war, nor did they question the validity of the conflict. They set out with courage and determination, not knowing what awaited them.

Nursing Sisters

Margaret Macdonald

When the war began, Margaret Macdonald was called from Kingston to Ottawa to succeed her older colleague, Georgina Pope, as matron of the Canadian Nursing Service. Her first assignment was to select and organize the nurses required to staff the two general hospitals, which were to accompany the first Canadian overseas contingent. Macdonald and her staff processed thousands of applications, interviewing promising candidates. When the mobilization order came through in mid-September, telegrams were sent to the one hundred successful applicants, instructing them to report to Quebec City on September 23. By this time Macdonald's offices had been relocated to Valcartier, Quebec. After a week filled with briefings, medical examinations, vaccinations and miles of paperwork, the embarkation orders finally arrived, and Macdonald and her nursing sisters set sail for Europe at the end of September.

The Armistice was signed on November 11, 1918. By May 1919, all overseas Canadian Medical units were disbanded. Macdonald, who received the Royal Red Cross from King George V and the Florence Nightingale Medal, returned to Canada in November 1919. She retired to Nova Scotia in 1923 but remained active, traveling extensively in Canada, the United States and Europe. When the Second World War broke out she again volunteered her services at age 66 but they were kindly refused. She died in 1948 in the house where she was born. She was given a funeral with full military honors.

Georgina Pope

Georgina Pope, the first Nursing Matron of the Canadian Nursing Service, who had served in the Boer War in South Africa and was the first Canadian to receive the Royal Red Cross for conspicuous service in the field, though no longer Matron, and denied overseas service because of her age, nonetheless made her mark in the First World War. For three years she worked to be allowed overseas service. Finally, in the summer of 1917, she got a posting. She was 55, which was considered much older then, when 60 was considered old, than it is now. She served at three English-based hospitals and then went to France. By August 1918, overwork and bombings had undermined her health. Pope officially retired in March 1919. When she died in 1938 her body lay in state in Government House and her military funeral was attended by veterans of both the Boer and First World wars.

GREEN DRAGON PRESS

No. 1 Canadian General Hospital, Etaples, France, 1918

Late on the evening of Sunday, May 19, 1918, fifteen German aircraft attacked Etaples, their ostensible target being the railway bridge which daily carried about a hundred military trains over the River Canche. The raid lasted two hours, during which 116 bombs were dropped indiscriminately over the many unprotected hospitals and reinforcement camps in the area. One of the bombs that fell within the lines of No. 1 Canadian General Hospital, leveling buildings or setting them ablaze, struck a wing of the nursing sisters' quarters, completely demolishing it. Nursing Sister Katharine Macdonald was killed instantly, and seven other sisters were wounded, two of these, N/S Gladys Wake and N/S Margaret Lowe, dying within a few days. To add to the horror, at least one enemy aeroplane, taking advantage of the bright moonlight and the glare from the burning huts, flew low and machine-gunned those engaged in rescue work.

The full toll of the night's casualties at No. 1 C.G.H. was 66 killed or to die of wounds, and 73 others wounded. Nearly half of those wounded were patients, and through the whole ghastly two hours that the raid continued, sisters went from hut to hut to attend them. The heavy casualties inflicted on the hospital's male staff had left the operating room without orderlies, but the nurses, assisted by some of the off-duty sisters, quickly prepared the theatre for action, covering the windows and doors with thick gray blankets. Here, surgeons and sisters toiled through the night dealing with cases in urgent need of surgery. Of the 1,156 patients in the wards when the enemy struck, 300 were suffering from fractured femurs. Anchored to their beds by immovable apparatus, they knew that the thin galvanized iron roof above them was no protection against bomb or bullet, and that the surrounding walls were largely of glass. In this nerve-racking situation they were greatly sustained by the presence of the nursing sisters, who stayed with them throughout the raid, encouraging and soothing them…. For their outstanding devotion to duty during the bombing, two of the staff, Nursing Sisters Helene Hanson and Beatrice McNair, became the first Canadian nurses in the war to be awarded the Military Medal…. Before May ended, the Etaples area had been hit by three more air raids. The worst, on May 31, completely wrecked the St. John Ambulance Brigade Hospital and caused heavy damage to No. 1 General…. After these further raids, NO. 1 C.G.H. and the St. John Ambulance Hospital were closed down. All patients were evacuated and nursing sisters assigned to other hospitals in France and England.

Canada's Nursing Sisters pp. 92,93.

GREEN DRAGON PRESS

BOMBS HIT TWO CANADIAN HOSPITALS

NURSES DISDAIN DEATH
TO HELP WOUNDED MEN

The bombing of a large hospital centre, which killed four Canadian nursing sisters, was first reported May 23, 1918. The contribution of Canadian women to the war effort was a key factor in women getting the vote in May, 1918.

Canadian Press Despatch

With the British Army in France — German airmen again have bombed heavily British hospitals in the area behind the lines and have killed and wounded some hundreds among the personnel and patients of many different hospitals in the group.

Recorded in the casualty list are the names of several sisters who, with other women nurses, stood bravely by their posts, throughout a terrific deluge of explosives.

This latest horror was perpetrated Sunday night, apparently by four squadrons of enemy planes which appear to have comprised more than a score of machines. A great number of bombs were dropped, about thirty per cent of them huge affairs which dug vast craters in the hospital grounds and the rest high-explosive shrapnel, which sent their death-dealing bullets tearing in every direction through the crowded hospital huts and buildings.

A three-seated airplane was brought down by gunfire while flying at a low altitude and the occupants were made prisoners. When questioned why he directed his men against hospitals, the captain explained, in a matter of fact way that he did not see the Red Cross signs. He said he was seeking military objectives and had no desire to molest hospitals.

Special Cable to The Star
by F. A. McKenzie

Hospital City in France, May 26 — I have just been hearing the brave simple tales of our nurses who escaped. No words would sufficiently emphasize one's sense of their splendid conduct.

The hospital city is a well-known district placed around a valley in a sandy channel near the coast, where a large number of temporary hospitals have been grouped together. Two big Canadian hospitals were there. These consisted of tents and huts. There were no bomb-proof shelters.

On Sunday evening there had been a concert. The sisters returning to quarters suddenly heard a loud humming and immediately one monster bomb fell direct upon the sleeping quarters of the Canadian orderlies and the other personnel. Many were blown to bits.

The enemy airman rained down bomb after bomb, some of small-calibre, solely man-killing bombs, others of a very large size. Two doctors, rushing to help, were caught by a bomb. One was killed and the other wounded. All the lights were immediately turned out except the little hand lamps with which the doctors and nursing sisters hastily sought to help the wounded. Sisters in night quarters were ordered to lie down under their beds.

The matron of No. 7 called two volunteers to move across the open under bomb fire and give needed help. Every sister present immediately volunteered. She took the nearest two, who moved out unhesitatingly, as though selected for a special honor.

One bomb fell among five sisters in quarter No. 1, killing one sister almost instantly and wounding five others, of whom one died shortly afterwards. The conduct of the patients, mostly British private soldiers, was magnificent. Their chief anxiety was lest the sisters should get hurt.

Margaret Lowe

A total of 3,141 nursing sisters served in the Canadian Army Medical corps in the Great War; 2,504 in England, France and the Eastern Mediterranean. Forty-six died during the Great War from drowning, disease and from shrapnel wounds suffered during air raids that struck field hospitals. Nursing Sister Margaret Lowe of Binscarth, Manitoba died of shrapnel wounds received during a German raid in France in May 1918.

On June 6, 1998, her great-niece Arlene Hill wrote an eloquent letter to the Toronto Star, excerpt below.

Nursing Sister Margaret Lowe. Photo courtesy Arlene Hill

Eighty years ago, my great-aunt, Margaret Lowe, was one of the four Canadian nurses killed at Canada's 1st General Hospital in France near the end of World War I. Another three died at the 3rd Stationary Hospital in unprecedented bombing raids on hospitals that previously had been considered exempt from attack.

Although I never knew her, I came upon her unexpectedly from time to time. In childhood, I discovered her service medals in the top drawer of my mother's dresser, next to her own nursing pins. I wanted those medals to enlarge on the slim story of how she had run from safety of tents and huts into the open area to help someone who was injured and, in doing so was fatally wounded herself....I am left to imagine if my great-aunt was one of the two volunteers selected to help the injured (every nurse volunteered but the matron chose the nearest two). Or, possibly, she ran to help the two doctors caught by a bomb while tending the injured (one killed, one wounded)....ultimately it doesn't matter. What does matter is that those women died the very month Canadian women received the right to vote. The major factor in granting that privilege was recognition of the contribution of women to Canada's war effort during World War I....Above all, our voting privilege is a gift from those nurses who died, whether on board a ship that was sunk, from illnesses contracted or, like those who died near the end of May, 1918, as direct casualties.

Surely we owe it to those who paid so dearly for our freedoms, to be constantly vigilant, to listen with discernment, and to exercise our franchise at each opportunity with care and gratitude.

ARLENE HILL
Peterborough

GREEN DRAGON PRESS

Casualty Form—Active Service.

M. F. W. 54. (A. F. B. 103.)
250M.—1-16.
H. Q. 1772-39-920.

Unit, Regiment or Corps _____ A M C T D No 10 _____

Regimental No. _Nurse_   Rank _Lieut_   Name _Lowe   Margaret_

Enlisted (a) _____ Terms of Service (a) _____ C.E.F. _____ Service reckons from (a) _____

Date of promotion to present rank. } _____ Date of appointment to lance rank } _____ Numerical position on roll of N.C.Os. } _____

Extended _____ Re-engaged _____ Qualification (b) _Prof. Nurse_

Date	From whom received	Record of promotions, reductions, transfers, casualties, etc., during active service, as reported on Army Form B 213, Army Form A. 36, or in other official documents. The authority to be quoted in each case.	Place	Date	Remarks taken from Army Form B. 213, Army Form A. 36, or other official documents.
		Embarked	Halifax	29.5.17	
		Disembarked	Liverpool	8.6.17	
25.6.17	A.M.C.	TAKEN ON STRENGTH	Westenhanger	29.5.17	Pt II D.O. 176
25.6.17	"	Posted to Ont Mil Hosp Orpington	Westenhanger	8.6.14	Pt II D.O. 176. Wr Webster Commanding C.A.M.C. DEPOT
23.6.17	O.M.H.	Taken on strength	Orpington	8.6.17	Pt.11.D.O.149.
5-12-17	1668 S.H.	Struck off strength to no 10 can Stat Hosp	Orpington	28-11-17	Pt. of D.O. 290 M M Crawford Major cams

---

Forms R. 150. E.T.
3232. 15 M.

Surname _LOWE_   Christian Names _Margaret_

Rank _Nursing Sister_   Name and Address of Next-of-Kin _Father._
Thomas Lowe.
Binscarth. Manitoba. Canada

Promotion _N S. 29.3.17_

Unit _Reinf. C.A.M.C. Nursing Sisters._

Place of birth _Mayshire. Scotland._ (or)

Married (Yes or No)

Appointments

Date of leaving Canada _7.9.5.17_   Date and Causes of Resignation

Date	From whom received	Record of Promotions, reductions, transfers, casualties, etc., during active service. The authority to be quoted in each case	Place	Date	REMARKS Taken from Official Documents
		T.O.S. camc CEF on arr 91 Can			
22.6.17	Dms.	& posted to camc Dep.		29.5.17	Co 799.
"	"	Posted to Ontario M.H.		8.6.17	Co 802.
8-10-17	DMS	Posted to No 16 Can Gen Orpington		5-10-17	CO 1310
4.12.17	do	Posted to No 10 Can Stat Hosp.		29.11.17	CO 1579
4.12.17	10 C.St.H.	SOS remaining for temp duty in England		8.12.17	
13.12.17	4 C.G.H.	Att temp duty		5.12.17	
29.1.18	Dms	Proc o'seas		26.1.18	
23.2.18	10 C.St.H.	arr in France 26.1.18 joined 10 C.St.H. 28.1.18			
16.3.18	do	SOS on rejoining to No 1 C.G.H.		8.3.18	
23.5.18	A.M.S.	Reported from Base wounded		19.5.18	
27.5.18	do	Adm 24 Gen Hosp Etaples		21.5.18	
29.5.18	do	Died of Wounds (from Air Raid)		28.5.18	
		1537			

Funeral of Sister Margaret Lowe of Binscarth, Manitoba, who died of shrapnel wounds received during a German air bombardment on the field hospital where she was stationed in Etaples, France, May 1918. Library and Archives Canada/Department of National Defence collection/PA-002575.

GREEN DRAGON PRESS

Ella Mae Bongard

Ella Mae Bongard of Picton, Ontario kept diaries during her service with a British medical unit at Etretat, France. Her son, Eric Scott, found her diaries in the attic and compiled them into a book, *Nobody Ever Wins a War*. These diaries vividly describe the struggle of caring for thousands of men injured in the mud and gore of the trenches. Ella Mae Bongard trained at one of the world's great hospitals, The Presbyterian Hospital in New York City. Following four years of training, she graduated in 1915, stayed in New York and practiced nursing for two years. Then she volunteered for overseas duty in the US Army Nursing Corps. She was sent to Etretat, on the Normandy coast. Her unit was less than 200 kilometers from the trenches. When she began her diaries, Ella Mae was a dedicated 26-year-old nurse, with a talent for observation. In her diaries we can see both the discipline of her training and the challenge of caring for hundreds of wounded soldiers. Ella Mae tried to maintain hope and optimism even when the situation seemed desperate. She never questioned the rightness of the Allied cause, though she did deplore the waste of lives.

Ella Mae Bongard
Courtesy Eric Scott family.

GREEN DRAGON PRESS

October 29, 1917
Had to relieve in Annex "C" and take care of the sick Germans. I'm glad it isn't my regular job for I can't help thinking how they treat our men who are prisoners, and I want to shoot them. However, I don't mind the real sick ones but I wouldn't trust the up patients at all. "C'est la guerre" you know.

November 12, 1917
Connie was gassed yesterday and leaves today for C.C.S.J.K. Davis went last week. I wish them luck. Had last hours and walked out to Benouville for dinner with Miss Geil and Miss Baker. Went by the cliff road, very dark and muddy. Had a delicious dinner and walked home by the main road.

November 14, 1917
The war news is pretty bad these days. The Germans seem to be walking right into Italy and Dr. Brewer and some who have come from Paris say that the people there are much alarmed. It is the most critical time in the war so far.

November 16, 1917
An air raid was reported last night & all the lights in the hospital were extinguished until daylight. They even say Havre was attacked but it is only rumour. However we are expecting one as most of the hospitals in this section have been bombed recently. A big convoy of 15 ships went past today escorted by two dirigibles. It is a frequent sight.

December 2, 1917
No time for diaries this past week. Had a big unexpected convoy Tuesday a.m. about 460 patients. They were right from the battle of Cambrai and such wounds as I've never seen. There were so many bad cases that even the medical wards had to be filled with surgical cases. We have worked madly all day with no time off except for hurried meals. I really enjoy being busy but oh how my back and feet ache at night. I'm sure I climb those three flights of stairs a million times a day helping with dressings. We do dressings nearly all day for the wounds are so large and take so long. Most of the men are regular bricks and don't scream even when you know you must be hurting them horribly. One little boy of 19 has had to have his leg amputated since he came here and another his right hand. They are both angels and it seems such a pity. Twelve new German prisoners, also from the battle of Cambrai were admitted to "C." I was sent in to help out. They are in pretty bad condition too & I felt pretty sorry for them until I went back in "D" and saw the poor "Tommies." If it weren't for the Germans they would all be strong healthy men.
One German fellow about 22 has the Iron Cross. He also is minus his right arm poor devil. I've never realized the war so much until this last convoy. I wonder if it's ever going to end. It seems so senseless to keep sending well men up the line to be shot to pieces. We have a case of tetanus. I've never seen one before & it's horrible to see him twitch & his jaw get rigid. I don't see how he can get better....

GREEN DRAGON PRESS

March 18, 1918
In bed all day and looking a lovely pale green shade. Personally I think I was "gassed"" from the last convoy. Who knows? Anyway I hope it doesn't repeat like the trench fever. This is the third time I've been off sick in a month.

March 31, 1918
The war is looking very serious indeed. Last night we got a convoy of 400 terribly wounded cases. They are right from the front as the C.C.S.'s have been either captured or destroyed. Thirty-four British sisters, refugees from the C.C.S.'s came down too. They are to stay here until they get somewhere to go so we are crowded in the "mess."

April 6 & 7, 1918
Sixteen more sisters have arrived here from Philadelphia unit at La Tréport. They had to evacuate. Things were getting too hot. The sea is our next move I guess. I wonder if the people at home know just how serious things have become over here. I refuse to believe that the worst can happen, but even if it should I prefer to stay and "stick it" than to have stayed at home in safety. No bravado or hero stuff intended just a plain statement of facts. I want to be in the midst of things that's all and so does everyone else here.

July 5, 1918
My birthday but no excitement. I didn't remember it until I went to date the night report.

July 24, 1918
Someone heard from the mobile unit today. They say they are working day and night even in the dugouts. They have had to move three times on account of being bombed. Sounds exciting. Wish I were there.

November 11, 1918
Today the Armistice was signed!! We can't believe it. Everyone is so excited that the work is in a mix up. The patients (The up ones) can get in the cafés now and are making up for lost time. We marched through the village streets at night carrying lighted torches and with our army capes inside out to show the scarlet lining. The French people kissed us on both cheeks as is customary here. It is hard to believe that the awful slaughter is over after four years.

Nobody Ever Wins a War.
Reprinted with permission, Eric Scott family.

GREEN DRAGON PRESS

Elizabeth Smellie

Some nurses served in both World Wars. Elizabeth Smellie was one of these. She was born at Port Arthur, Ontario, 22 March 1884. She graduated from the Johns Hopkins Training School for Nurses in Baltimore, Maryland, and when The First World War broke out she joined the Canadian Army Nursing service. Elizabeth Smellie served and was awarded medals in Britain and France, and after the war was appointed assistant matron in chief, serving with Margaret Macdonald. Later she helped build the Victorian Order of Nurses and was its chief superintendent from 1923 to 1947. She also served in World War II, laid the foundations for the Canadian Women's Army Corps, and in 1944 became the first women colonel in the Canadian army.

Medal set, Colonel Elizabeth Smellie, Royal Red Cross 1914-1915 Star; British War Medal, 1914-1919; Victory Medal, 1914-1919; Oak Leaf; Canadian Volunteer Service Medal; War Medal, 1939-1045; King George V Jubilee Medal; and Canadian Centennial Medal.
Canadian War Museum, 20000105-049.

GREEN DRAGON PRESS

Charlotte Edith Anderson Monture

Edith Anderson was remarkable for several reasons. She was a nurse, a woman on active duty, and an officer — probably the first woman officer nurse. Beyond all that, though, she was from the Six Nations and was one of about 2000 First Nations people to serve in the war. This is extraordinary because First Nations people were exempted from service; all who went did so voluntarily.

Denied admission to Canadian nursing schools, Edith was accepted at the New Rochelle [New York] Hospital School of Nursing in 1914. Working as a public health and school nurse in New York City when the United States entered the First World War in 1917, she volunteered as a Nursing Sister with the American Expeditionary Force's Army Medical Corps. A caring and compassionate woman, she wrote in her journal about the death of a patient who had adopted her as his "big sister":

"My heart was broken. Cried most of the day and could not sleep…."

Following service at the U.S. Army Base Hospital 23 in Vittel, France, Anderson returned home to the Six Nations Reserve in 1919. She married Claybran Monture, raised a family, and continued working as a nurse and midwife until her retirement in 1955. She died on the reserve in 1996, shortly before her 106th birthday.

On All Frontiers: Four Centuries of Canadian Nursing, p. 86.

Public Relations

Nurses who returned to Canada during the war on furlough or accompanying wounded soldiers were in great demand as speakers. In 1917, The *Renfrew Mercury* reported the presentation by Nursing Sister Sarah Payne to a gathering of Red Cross members.

"Nursing Sister Sarah Payne, who was trained as a nurse in Kingston and began war duty in August, 1915, recently arrived back on this side of the Atlantic as one of the nurses on shipboard in charge of a group of convalescing wounded soldiers. She was permitted a few days furlough to come home to see her father, arriving on Thursday. Learning of her presence here some of the Red Cross officials felt it might help their work if they could meet one who had actually been using Red Cross supplies. Though her time was limited, having to return on the Saturday night train, she kindly consented.

"On Saturday afternoon the trim little nurse in her military uniform of dark blue, with brass buttons, red collar and red stripes, faced an audience of some forty Red Cross members.

"Miss Payne said that of late the nurses had had to make their own surgical dressings. Why, she could not tell. An interesting sidelight was the statement that the men greatly appreciated the 'comfort bags' of the Red Cross. Also that they were so few in number – only five on the boat she had come on – that they raffled them, not for money but just to decide who should be the lucky few out of the many. There were 168 patients and two nursing sisters on board.

"The preferred nightshirts, she said, were of ordinary rectory cotton. These stood the washing better. Some Canadian women had made shirts to tie at the back and mistaking the use of these had put a pocket in the back, leading some of the men to say that people in Canada must be quite limber. It was protested that these gowns were not from Renfrew!

"Miss Payne said that any tobacco sent to wounded soldiers in English hospitals had to pay duty. She had handled parcels with a little tobacco in them and had had to pay duty on the whole weight of the parcel.

"That night Miss Payne again sent her face seaward. It appears that every nurse is supposed to take her turn at duty on board ship, for a term of at least three ships."
The *Renfrew Mercury*, 1917.

GREEN DRAGON PRESS

Nursing Sisters Who Lost their Lives in World War I

1915
Matron Jaggard, Jessie Brown, 3rd Stationery Hospital
N/S Munro, Mary Frances E., 3rd Stationery Hospital

1916
N/S Nourse, Grace E Boyd, Canadian Army Military Corp (CAMC)
N/S Ross, Elsie Gertrude, Canadian Army Military Corp (CAMC)
N/S Tupper Addie Allen (Adruenna), Royal Red Cross (RRC)CAMC

1917
N/S Garbutt, Sarah Ellen (Ontario Military Hospital)
N/S Sparks, Letitia (7 General Hospital)

1918
N/S Alpaugh, Agnes Estelle, CAMC
N/A Alport (Roberts), Jean Ogilvie (4 General Hospital)
N/S Baker, Miriam Eastman (15 General Hospital)
N/S Baldwin, Dorothy Mary Yarwood (3 Stationery Hospital)
N/S Bartlett, Bertha (Newfoundland Voluntary Aid Detachment)
N/S Campbell, Christina (5 General Hospital)
N/S Dagg, Ainslie St. Clair (15 General Hospital)
N/S Davis, Len A. (4 General Hospital)
N/S Douglas, Carola Josephine, CAMC (H.S.)
N/S Dussault, Alexina, CAMC (H.S)
N/S Follette, Minnie Asenath, CAMC (H.S.)
N/S Forneri, Agnes Florien (8 General Hospital)
N/S Fortescue, Margaret Jane, CAMC (H.S.)
Matron Fraser, Margaret Majory, CAMC (H.S.)
N/S Frederickson, Christine, CAMC
N/S Gallaher, Minnie Katherine, CAMC (H.S.)
N/S Green, Matilda Ethel (7 General Hospital)
N/S Hennan, Victoria Belle (9 General Hospital)
N/S Hunt, Myrtle Margaret, CAMC
N/S Jarvis, Jessie Agnes, CAMC
N/S Jenner, Lenna Mae, CAMC
N/S Kealy, Ida Lilian (1 General Hospital)
N/S Lowe, Margaret (1 General Hospital
N/S McDiarmid, Jessie Mabel (5 General Hospital)
N/S MacDonald, Katherine Maud (1 General Hospital)
N/S MacEachen, Rebecca Helen, CAMC
N/S McKay, Eveln Verrall (3 General Hospital)
N/S McKenzie, Mary Agnes, CAMC (H.S.)
N/S McLean, Rena, R.R.C. (2 Stationery Hospital)
N/S MacPherson, Agnes, R.R.C. (3 Stationery Hospital)
N/S Mellett, Henrietta, (15 General Hospital)
N/S Pringle, Eden Lyal, (3 Stationery Hospital)
N/S Rogers, Nellie Grace, CAMC

GREEN DRAGON PRESS

N/S Ross, Ada Janet (1 General Hospital)
N/S Sampson, Mary Belle, CAMC (H.S.)
N/S Sare, Gladys Irene, CAMC (H.S.)
N/S Stamers, Anna Irene, CAMC (H.S.)
N/S Templeman, Jean, CAMC (H.S.)
N/S Trusdale, Alice L., CAMC
N/S Twist, Dorothy Pearson (Canadian Military V.A.D.)
N/S Wake, Gladys Maude Mary (1 General Hospital)
N/S Whitely, Anna Elizabeth, 10 Stationery Hospital

1919
N/S Baker, Margaret Elisa, CAMC
N/S Champagne, Ernestine (8 General Hospital)
N/S Donaldson (Petty), Gertrude (1 General Hospital)
N/S Grant, Grace Mabel, CAMC
N/S King, Jessie Nelson (1 General Hospital)
N/S McDougal, Agnes (10 Stationery Hospital)
N/S McIntosh, Rebecca (9 General Hospital)
N/S MacLeod, Margaret Christine (2 General Hospital)

1920
N/S McGinnis, Mary Geraldine, CAMC

1921
N/S Cumming, Isobel Katherine (1 General Hospital)
N/S Hanna, Bessie Maud (3 Stationery Hospital)

1922
N/S Green, Caroline Graham, CAMC (H.S.)

Note: Spelling as in original
http://www.vac-acc.gc.ca/general/sub.cfm?source=history/other/Nursing/ward

GREEN DRAGON PRESS

Medical Doctors

From the moment that women were finally admitted to the study of medicine, they were subjected to embarrassing ordeals during their training. The major objection to medical training for women was the issue of co-education, especially when the subject was the human body. Male students and faculty, unable to accept women in their midst, harassed and intimidated them during anatomy classes with vulgar drawings and demonstrations. Given the challenges faced and overcome by Canadian women who wanted to study medicine, it is not surprising that the women doctors who served at the Front performed amazing acts of courage and endurance. Dr. Irma LeVasseur and Dr. Mary Lee Edward were two outstanding examples.

Dr. Irma LeVasseur

Dr. Irma LeVasseur was born in Quebec City in 1878, the daughter of the journalist Louis-Nazaire LeVasseur. She was educated in a convent and had decided at an early age on a career in medicine. Her problem was where to study. Neither Laval University nor the Université de Montréal accepted women, nor did McGill University. The hospital attached to Bishop's University was so anti-woman that it was hardly worthwhile to try to enroll. Irma spoke English as well as French, and rather than choosing a Canadian university she applied to and was accepted at the Minnesota University College of Medicine at St. Paul. After practicing in New York City, she returned to Montreal, where she embarked on an extremely successful career in paediatric medicine before she gained fame for her work in World War I.

Dr. LeVasseur volunteered in April 1915 and left for Europe with four other doctors, all male. Her posting was in Serbia, where the population was being ravaged by a typhus epidemic that claimed 300,000 lives before it ran its course. Typhus had arrived in Serbia with the invading Austrian army, and though the Austrians had been driven back, the disease remained.

Dr. LeVasseur worked day and night under constant enemy bombardment, organizing an immunization program and treating the wounded as well as the sick. When the Germans invaded, Dr. LeVasseur had to withdraw her unit to avoid capture. She set up another hospital 30 miles back but there was virtually no food and soon medicine ran out. Although the situation was desperate, she kept on going through exhaustion and frustration. Worse was to come. Serbia fell and a Great Retreat began. Hospital units, diplomats, Serbian soldiers, thousands of near-starving men, women and children fled toward safety. It is estimated that more than 700,000 people died on the journey. Dr. LeVasseur made it to the coast, surviving her ordeal to return to Canada to resume her work.

Those Indomitable Lady Doctors, p. 185.

Dr. Mary Lee Edward

Dr. Mary Lee Edward, born in Petrolia, Ontario, graduated from the University of Toronto medical school in 1908, the only woman in a class of 150. She joined an American medical unit because she was working in New York when the war broke out.

Mary Lee had to move to New York because there was little opportunity for this ambitious young graduate in Canada. She organized an all-female medical team, arriving on the battlefield toward the end of the war, after the United States entered the conflict. She was in the first American unit to go overseas, and they went straight to France, only to discover their hospital had been destroyed. The unit was sent to the front just in time to deal with the results of the full German offensive. Their hospital was attacked from the air by bombs and strafed by machine gun fire. At times patients arrived by the hundreds, were wheeled on stretchers into the preparation room, to be cleaned of mud and grass by a nurse and then sent to surgery.

"On more than one occasion, when the doctors went off duty, they would realize that they had been working alongside a whole box of legs that they had amputated during the night. There wasn't time for any attention to delicacies, no time to talk of shielding ladies from the grosser side of life. Sometimes Dr. Edward operated for as long as sixty hours at a stretch, not pausing to sleep and hardly pausing to eat. Shells burst around her, bombs fell on the hospital (thirteen nurses killed, eleven wounded), and on she went, cutting and stitching.

"'Operated 12 midnight to 8 a.m.,' reads her diary. 'Operated 4.12 p.m.' There remained 100 wounded to operate on. At times there are 400 or more arriving all the time….Boche advancing….Operating now with three equips….Evacuating and operating on high speed. Some on tables four hours after wounded….Many evacuants from Compeigne….'
"She was exhausted, and yet there was no stopping. She couldn't stop as long

as the casualties kept coming in. And the casualties poured in until later in the year when at last the war turned in favour of the allies."

The Indomitable Lady Doctors, p. 185.

Dr. Edward survived the war. She and four colleagues were awarded the Croix de Guerre by the French Government at a special ceremony at the Front and on her return home the University of Toronto awarded her a Roll of Service in honor of her gallant work for King and Country. She practiced medicine until she was eighty-five. Before her death in 1980, she wrote notes for her memoirs, including her recollections of the sexist challenges of her anatomy class and the horrors she witnessed on the front.

From Dr. Edward's notes on classroom experience:

"Each day, they assembled 10 minutes before the lecture began and sat in their places. When I took my place, I was pelted with chalk, chalk brushes and assailed with catcalls and a song, Hop Along Sister Mary. I had to enter from the [door at the] front of the amphitheatre, climb 30 or 40 steps and sit at the back. At the end of the six-year course, in the spring of 1908, I won the George Brown Scholarship, the highest honour available in this course. It amounted to $350 and entitled one to a year's research work."

From her notes on the war:

"May 31, 1918: About 3 a.m., many more wounded arrived. One old lady was brought in with shrapnel in her head from a bomb and, by 8 a.m., 300 wounded had arrived. The whole sky was lit by a nearby village. Flames could be seen. Great numbers of wounded continued to arrive. Several teams were working. We worked from 3 a.m. to 2 p.m. After 2 p.m., we went on our round and performed dressings. Then we slept for one hour – from 10 p.m. to 11 p.m."

"All these cases were wounded by bullets, one with the lower half of his face shot away. An American sculptress in Paris would send to the soldier's home for a photograph and from this she would make a sculpture of his face. A famous plastic surgeon in Paris would then build up his face."

Electric Library Canada - Document

Canadian Red Cross ambulance
City of Toronto Archives, Fonds 1244, Item 885.

Voluntary Aid Detachment (VADs)

"Britain set up Voluntary Aid Detachments (VADs) and sent thousands of hastily trained nurses and orderlies to work in military hospitals. The VAD nurses generally acted as assistants to the professional military nurses (also known as nursing sisters), and therefore carried out unpleasant but essential nursing tasks such as emptying bedpans and getting rid of soiled dressings.

The VAD women generally came from upper- and middle-class British families, and were at least twenty-three years old. They felt they were doing their part for the war effort by performing unpaid menial work that, a few months earlier, would have been considered far beneath them.

When the Battle of the Somme ended in November of 1916, the British armies had suffered over 420,000 casualties, 25,000 of them Canadian. With such staggering losses, more and more men were required at the Front to replace battle casualties. Suddenly, new jobs opened up for women. At the start of the war, the job of driving Red Cross ambulances had been considered too dangerous and exhausting for women; indeed, few women knew how to drive motor vehicles. But now VADs recruited women to replace the male ambulance drivers who had been sent to fight at the Front."
HERStory III: Women from Canada's Past, p. 144.

Jane Walters

Jane Walters, daughter of a newspaper owner in Welland, Ontario, recalled her experiences as a VAD in a military hospital in London:
"It was difficult as a VAD getting used to the English sisters. That was very hard. The discipline in a British military hospital was something! We had our meals in a vast room, part of the original building. You went down steps into it, and it was long, and towards the other end you went up steps, and there's where the lord and lady of the manor would sit in the olden days. You remember the saying 'below the salt'. You went down steps and all the tables here were for the nursing sisters and the VADs. The matron and the entire senior nursing sisters and the heads of the hospital would be up there. The matron only came to second dinner, and when she would come, the VAD who was sitting at the end of that table, the nearest to the door through which she would come, would get up and go to the door and hold the door open. When the matron would come in, you'd have to give her a little bow."

"We didn't grumble – the hierarchy didn't affect us. Some of the nursing sisters in charge of each ward were very strict. Some of them I couldn't bear. One of them was so rude to me one day that I just turned round and sauced her back. I said, 'I haven't come 3,000 miles to work voluntarily to be spoken to like that by anybody.' Of course she reported me to the matron and I was up on the carpet. So I was changed from that ward."

"My experience as a VAD certainly broadened me. You met people from all over the world. You did things you never thought you were going to do. And you had stern discipline, and you had hardship – terrible things to look at, to see, and to do, and you had to just grit your teeth and do it. It was a wonderful character builder." *The Great War and Canadian Society,* p. 125.

GREEN DRAGON PRESS

Grace MacPherson Livingston

Grace MacPherson worked as a volunteer Red Cross ambulance driver at the huge "hospital city" of Etaples, France. She worked 12 hour shifts driving ambulances full of wounded men over bumpy dirt roads for 14 shillings a week. Grace continued to perform her duty to the best of her ability throughout the war and escaped injury when Etaples was bombed during a number of air attacks in 1918. Many other nurses and orderlies were killed or wounded. Grace was described as "the bravest of them all" for her calm work during those horrific times. At first, Grace experienced some difficulty coping with the extremely strict discipline imposed on the VADs. Her naturally breezy nature did not fit well with the tight restrictions. The VADs could go to tea with officers but were not allowed to dine with them unless chaperoned. Dancing with men would lead to instant dismissal. Grace was constantly reprimanded for improper behaviour and incorrect dress. Even though she was miserable she persevered and the situation improved. She eventually made friends.

In *HERStory III*, Susan Merritt wrote about Grace:
Grace MacPherson, the youngest of six children, was born in Winnipeg, Manitoba, 1895. While she was still a child, her family moved to Vancouver, British Columbia. Her father, a civil engineer, died soon after the move. Grace was a popular young woman with a sparkling personality that attracted many friends. Like other 'nice' women of the times, she taught Sunday School, took an active part in her church youth group and went to dances and the moving picture shows. She also had a rebellious streak, and at eighteen, rather than go straight from her mother's house into marriage, Grace attended Business College. There she studied typing and shorthand. Clerical work had been dominated by men in the 1800s and even by 1911 less than one out of every three Canadian clerical workers was female. Yet Grace daringly looked forward to "going out to business" and getting an office job.

A few years later, Grace, employed as a secretary, astonished Vancouver and became one of the first women in the city to own her own car. She proudly dashed about in her Paige Detroit, changing her own tires and dealing with troublesome road hogs.

[At first] the war did not rock the world of Grace MacPherson. Canadians wanted to show the world how well they could fight, and it was exciting when Grace's male friends proudly wore their new uniforms. But no one expected the war to last long. And no one expected to die. Her brother Alex had not even waited to join Vancouver's local 72nd Battalion. Instead, he had rushed off to England and enlisted as a lieutenant in the Highland Light Infantry. Grace did not worry about Alex, for he had always been lucky. But her brother's luck ran out in Turkey. In September of 1915, Grace learned by telegram that Alex had died of wounds at Gallipoli. For Grace, war no longer meant handsome uniforms; it meant injury and it meant death.

Grace came up with a plan. Alex had already died in the war and so had one of her boyfriends. Like so many Canadian women, she longed to do more to help "the boys" overseas. Her diary, begun at the age of eighteen, indicates that a few weeks later she wrote to the Red Cross and volunteered her services as an ambulance driver. In France, the ambulance drivers drove wounded soldiers between the hospital trains, the hospitals, and ships sailing for England. Grace did not receive encouraging replies but decided to travel to England in hopes of obtaining such a position. For the next two months, she spent her lunch hours pestering the Canadian Pacific Steamship Office for a free passage overseas. As Grace pointed out, the male volunteers received free passage, so why shouldn't she? The Vancouver office finally gave in, and chaperoned by an elderly Vancouver couple, Grace sailed for England. Sailing during the wartime was in itself an act of courage; a year earlier, on 7 May 1915, the Lusitania had been sunk by German U-boats in sight of Ireland, and 1,198 had perished.

When Germany invaded Belgium in August of 1914, King George V, on behalf of the British Empire, declared war, Canada, as part of the British Empire, was committed to take part in what was expected to be a short and glorious war.

But the war quickly turned into a bloody standoff in the trenches and battlefields of Belgium and France (the Western Front). When Grace arrived in London in 1916, everyone realized this war would be neither short nor glorious. The "improved" weapons of this war were killing and maiming at an incredible rate. On average, infantry soldiers would last only one year in combat before being killed or seriously wounded. Military medical services were struggling to care for vast numbers of wounded soldiers.

After the Battle of the Somme, the VADs took over ambulance duty at Etaples, France, a small fishing port, which had been transformed into a medical receiving centre of over forty thousand hospital beds. This huge military hospital complex was located sixteen kilometers (ten miles) south of Boulogne on the English Channel.

When Grace arrived in London, she rushed to VAD headquarters to obtain a position as an ambulance driver. On 28 March 1917 an excited Grace received her marching orders. She was one of twenty women sent to reinforce the ambulance convoy at Etaples, France. Altogether about one hundred women worked as ambulance drivers during the war, and Grace was one of four Canadian women chosen. There were, in addition, two Newfoundland women drivers. Newfoundland was still a separate self-governing British colony, and the fiercely proud Newfoundlanders were not classed as Canadians.

Grace rushed around London putting together her kit. As a volunteer, she had to pay for her own uniform. Ambulance drivers were usually exposed to the weather as they drove, so she bought a leather coat, high-laced boots, an aviator helmet and lots of warm underwear…. Grace crossed the English Channel and arrived in a snow storm at Etaples on 8 April 1917. The next day, Canadian forces had their greatest victory when they captured Vimy Ridge – at a cost of over ten thousand casualties in six days.

A soldier who was wounded at the Front was first treated at his battalion's Field Dressing Station. If the wounds required more care, he was then moved to a Casualty Clearing Station which was always located on a railway line. The Casualty Clearing Stations often had emergency operating huts to deal with wounds requiring early treatment. If the wounded soldier could be treated at a general hospital, he was placed on one of the row of shelves inside the hospital train and transported to Etaples. At Etaples, Red Cross

GREEN DRAGON PRESS

ambulance drivers such as Grace met the hospital trains. Stretcher bearers or orderlies loaded the wounded into ambulances. Then the ambulance drivers delivered the men to the appropriate general hospitals at Etaples. It was called a convoy when ambulance drivers moved wounded men from the trains. If a wounded man was being sent back to England, an ambulance picked him up at the hospital and either drove him back to the train station or else drove him directly to one of the hospital ships at Boulogne. This was called an evacuation. Each convoy and each evacuation took about three hours.

Grace worked twelve-hour shifts either from 8:00 am to 8:00 pm, or from 8:00 pm to 8:00 am. A typical shift included one convoy and one evacuation over bumpy dirt roads that were slick and greasy when wet. However when huge numbers of wounded men arrived after a battle such as Vimy Ridge, the ambulance drivers might work forty-eight hours at a stretch, with only a few hours of sleep. All this was done for no pay, for although Grace and the other Red Cross drivers had the honorary title of lieutenant, they did not receive a salary. Instead, the women, as volunteers, received fourteen shillings a week to put towards mess and laundry expenses.

Grace noted in her small pocket diary that the ambulances were in poor condition when the male ambulance drivers turned them over to the VADs. Grace and the other drivers were each responsible for the maintenance of two or three ambulances. These were clumsy, bulky McLaughlin Buicks donated by public-spirited organizations. Each day at noon, the Commandant closely inspected the vehicles. Every ambulance had a vehicle number, and the driver was identified by that number....

In March of 1918, the German army launched a series of attacks which won them huge areas of France. As Germany smashed through Allied lines, more and more hospital trains pulled into Etaples bearing the shattered bodies of wounded men. By April, the Front had moved closer to Etaples. There was a never-ending crash and thud of guns, and at night the sky lit up with the flash of bursting shells. Nurses, hastily evacuated from captured Casualty Clearing Stations, sought shelter in Etaples. Train and truck traffic was even heavier than usual, rushing ammunition and other supplies toward the ever-approaching Front. Grace and the others worked longer and longer hours. Exhausted, they struggled to keep awake at the wheel as they drove more wounded men to the overcrowded hospitals....The clear and moonlit evening of Sunday, 19 May 1918, was a perfect night for an air raid. German aircraft, attempting to destroy railway lines and supply trains, dropped 116 torpedoes and incendiaries on Etaples's unprotected hospitals and camps. There were over a thousand patients in the hospital wards when the two-hour raid began.

Male staff quarters at No. 1 Canadian General Hospital were hit, and there were heavy casualties. Parts of the military nurses' quarters were also demolished and three nurses died while five others were wounded. No. 7 Canadian General Hospital was also hit, with some casualties. During the air raid, Grace and the other drivers took shelter from the flying debris under their beds; miraculously, none were injured. When the raid was over, the women quickly set to work. The devastating raid had caused about 750 casualties and many orderlies had been wounded or killed. The drivers transported the wounded to operating rooms and did whatever else had to be done on that horrific night in May.

GREEN DRAGON PRESS

Grace wrote that RA660 (her vehicle) performed well, but did not write about her part in the aftermath. One captain, however, described her as "a very gritty woman," and wrote that while some of the men were panic-stricken, Grace, first on the scene with her ambulance, "worked all night without a quiver." Before the end of May the Etaples area endured three more air attacks. No. 1 Canadian General Hospital and the St. John Ambulance Brigade Hospital were so damaged that their patients were evacuated and the two hospitals closed.

Grace MacPherson as a Voluntary Aid Detachment (VAD) driver for the British Red Cross on June 8, 1917. This photograph and others were taken for the Canadian War Photographs exhibition at the fashionable Grafton Galleries in central London, and appeared on the front page of The *Canadian News Record*, which was published by the War Records Office. Library and Archives Canada/Department of National Defence collection/PA-001305.

Grace left Etaples late in the summer of 1918. For over a year she had worked at a dangerous and grueling job for fourteen shillings a week. She was running out of money and she needed a change. Using her secretarial skills, she briefly worked for the wife of the Canadian High Commissioner. Then she earned her living as head driver at an American military hospital in London. In late 1919 she returned to Vancouver and found employment at the Department of Soldiers' Civil Re-establishment. Shortly thereafter, handsome Major David Livingston saw Grace across the room at a veterans' dance. He swept an astonished Grace up into his arms and declared that she was the one that he would marry. David Livingston was a civil engineer in charge of building branch lines for the Canadian Pacific Railway. He and Grace were married the following spring, and Grace lived in the wilderness of northern British Columbia for much of her early married life….Justly proud of her own wartime contribution, Grace always insisted on marching with the men in Remembrance Day parades. Grace MacPherson Livingston died in Vancouver in 1979.

Excerpted from *HERStory III: Women from Canada's Past*, by Susan Merritt. Reprinted with permission.

GREEN DRAGON PRESS

The Belgian Canal Boat Fund

Mabel Cawthra, a member of one of Toronto's richest and most powerful families, was talented, intelligent and handsome. She had studied painting and sculpture and travelled in Europe, India and Japan. In 1900, against her mother's wishes, Mabel married Agar Adamson. In the years before the war, she raised a family and ran an interior design business. When her husband volunteered and was sent overseas, the ambitious and adventurous Mabel was not content to stay at home making the rounds of society parties. She followed her husband to England.

Her decision was not that unusual for the times. By 1917, according to one estimate, about 30,00 Canadian wives and sweethearts had arrived in England, mainly for social reasons. But Mabel was not interested in the social scene and was determined to make a difference. She took trunk-loads of clothes with her, collected from fashionable houses in Toronto, to distribute to Belgian refugees in England.

Mabel's mother had a flat in London, with central heating, two servants, a car and chauffeur. In the beginning, Mabel got her son settled in boarding school while waiting for the right opportunity, took wounded Belgian soldiers for outings, completed an intensive course in nursing and practised the French she had learned as an art student in Paris. She also continued to deal with the shipments of clothing that arrived from Toronto.

Finding the perfect project proved difficult. Many organizations in support of the war were often in conflict with each other. She tried volunteering her car and herself as chauffeur for ambulance duty. Her car was accepted but she was turned down. Mabel recognized that being a woman was a disadvantage, and that only nurses were taken seriously. In July 1915, suffrage societies organized a march of 30,000 women in London demanding their right to be employed in the war effort. (*Tapestry of War*, p. 124). Later, as more men were conscripted, labour shortages became serious, prejudice against women lessened, and then the tide turned, with the government exhorting women to fill the places of men.

Mabel's easiest option would have been to work in the female surroundings of the Canadian Red Cross Society, but she wanted to make her mark in a more significant and personal way. Now that the basic needs of Belgian refugees in England had been met, Mabel thought about those who had stayed behind in the small part of Belgium still in Allied hands. This was a narrow strip of land running from the coast to the city of Ypres. Thousands of families lived here within range of the guns. All food and clothing were in short supply. It was a chance meeting with an acquaintance from Toronto that inspired the idea of using a canal barge to deliver food and other necessities along the web of waterways of the area.

With her organizational skills, social contacts, and of course money, Mabel soon got the project underway. A high-powered honorary committee and a rented office gave the venture professional status. They then had to convince the Belgian government that the project was a viable one and obtain visas so the staff could cross the channel. Mabel wrote to her mother that "We are going to interview the

Belgian government....They evidently think we have the whole of Canada behind us, which is a little disconcerting, but I have hope that Canada will back me up" (*Tapestry of War*, p. 128).

The Belgian Canal Boat Fund was refused permission to operate in the war zone but finally established headquarters on the outskirts of the medieval market town of Furnes, near a school. For the next four years they fed and clothed all 370 students at the school as well as distributing food and clothing to hundreds of refugees. They also established a medical clinic and a pharmaceutical dispensary. The American businessman Herbert Hoover, later US president, and at the time London-based chairman of the American Committee for Belgian relief, was supportive of the project, helping with the shipping of supplies from England to Belgium.

Late in the second year of the project, Mabel decided to commission a fund-raising poster. Competition among the different charities was fierce so Mabel knew the poster would have to be dramatic. She hired one of the best commercial artists, John Hassall, whose art had made Colman's Mustard famous. The poster, an outstanding example of propaganda art, is still attractive to contemporary eyes. *Tapestry of War*, p. 131.

Mabel spent much of her time at Furnes, frequently under air raid, and within shelling range of enemy guns. She was able to turn a group of young society debutantes into a disciplined team of relief workers, while at the same time learning to deal with the values of those who were being helped.

Although Mabel's husband was supportive of her work and often visited Furnes, the stresses both faced were beginning to place a strain on the marriage.

He resented the time she gave to her project and she disliked his constant requests for her to do errands and provide for his needs, most of which she saw as frivolous (for example, he asked her to send him paté from Fortnum and Mason, real clotted cream from Devonshire, silk underwear,

GREEN DRAGON PRESS

wigs and costumes for the regimental comedy company). Both were absorbed in what they were doing, so the doings of the other became an intrusion. When Mabel refused to return to London where Agar was to be invested by King George V with the Distinguished Service Order medal, because, she said, there was too much work to do, Agar was very angry. Eventually, though, he cooled off. Mabel was physically exhausted at the time and became seriously ill. She had also begun suffering an inflammation of the eyes that affected her appearance and made reading and writing difficult. Sometime in 1917, suffering severe internal pain, she collapsed at Furnes and had to be sent home by ambulance. Cancer was suspected and in February of 1918, knowing that Agar's regiment was out of the line, she wrote to him. He rushed back to England and resigned his commission. Mabel had a serious operation, and while the cause of her illness is not known, it was not cancer. She recovered quickly, and later returned to Furnes. Agar Adamson was unable to rejoin the Princess Patricia's, but a staff job was found for him behind the lines.

The couple's post-war life was not happy. They went to Bruges in Belgium and then returned in the autumn to Canada and a beautiful new house on their Port Credit property. Agar seemed to be suffering from some kind of shell shock. He became impatient and irritable. Cars made him jumpy and he quarreled with taxi drivers and blew up at waiters in restaurants and at his own servants. That he could not find useful employment caused great discord between them. By the early 20s, Agar spent much time away from home, in Ottawa and England. In the fall of 1929, he survived a crash in an experimental plane. But the two hours he spent in the Irish Sea hanging onto the wreckage was too much for him and he died two months later. Despite the many years they had been estranged, Mabel arranged the kind of funeral Agar would have wanted. The Royal Canadian Regiment served as an honor guard, the casket was placed on a gun carriage and followed by three pipers, a company of the local militia regiment and a riderless horse with empty boots reversed in the stirrups. Many veterans of the Princess Patricia's Canadian Light Infantry were present.

Mabel lived on in Port Credit, always active in promoting the arts and in community activities. She died there in 1943.

Based on the story of Mabel Adamson in *Tapestry of War* by Sandra Gwyn, HarperCollins, 1992.

All Work and No Play…

With so many young people far from home, it was understandable that romance would seem important in such desperate times when the future was unknown.

Jane Walters recalls:

"Patients had a habit of falling in love with you. They were so glad to get back home and have young girls around who weren't too hard to look at and who were kind, who helped them. I remember there was one Roumanian soldier, and he thought he was in love with me. I kinda thought I was in love with him too. He was very attractive. You know, a girl who has ideals – and we had ideals in those days, I hope you have now – to be thrown in with men like that, all kinds from all over the world, it took some doing to keep level, not have your head turned. But you had your heart hurt very often."

And Anita White Phillips remembers being teased because pilots dropped notes as they buzzed the hospital:

"We had a doctor on our ward, Dr. Robertson, I think it was. He'd been there for quite a long time, and I had been there for a long time too. And he came in one morning, and he said, 'Have we got Nursing Sister White?' We all looked so amazed at him. I said, 'Why, of course. What's the matter?' He says, 'Well, you tell your boyfriends that are flying over this place to stop dropping bombs on my head.' They had little things that they put weights on, and they put a note inside it, and they dropped them. He happened to be passing, and it dropped right on his head….The notes told me where they had been, and when they'd be back, and hope you'd be at a little dance, or something like that. Just nice notes."

The Great War and Canadian Society,
p. 148.

Canadian women's wartime experiences changed their lives in ways most of them never expected. The survivors came home to a changed world. Particularly in Europe and in North America, life would never be the same.

The Canadian military medical services soon reverted to their prewar status. When post-war reorganization was complete, the Royal Canadian Army had a permanent staff of only eight nursing sisters. By 1922 all nursing sisters who had served in the war had been demobilized. Nonetheless, some of the women who had provided medical care at home and overseas took their experiences and built careers in medicine.

For many women, marriage and family were not an option, because tens of thousands of men died during the conflict. Most of those who had served did not speak of what they observed and survived. Their diaries were packed away with uniforms and medals and only came to light many years after the end of the terrible conflict. The diaries of Clare Gass and Ella Mae Bongard and the stories of other women speak to us of young people going off cheerfully and bravely, never suspecting what horrors they would face. They met the challenge, serving with great courage and distinction. Some of them would never return

Each woman's story is different and all the stories share the backdrop of misery and heroism, excitement and boredom, life at its most vivid heights and at its most drab depths. Millions died in World War I and the war changed every one of the millions of people who had been even remotely involved.

GREEN DRAGON PRESS

Chapter 4: Afterword

Last Pay, Munitions Factory.
City of Toronto Archives, Fonds 1244, Item 924.

When the war ended, women were urged to return to their homes to make way for returning servicemen. Below is one of the many propaganda bulletins that were issued by the Ontario Government. Some, like this one, were directed to female employees, others to their employers.

TO WOMEN WORKERS

Are you working for love or for money?

Are you holding a job you do not need?

Perhaps you have a husband well able to support you and a comfortable home?

You took a job during the war to help meet the shortage of labour.

You have "Made good" and you want to go on working.

But the war is over and conditions have changed.

There is no longer a shortage of labour. On the contrary Ontario is faced by a serious situation due to the number of men unemployed.

This number is being increased daily by returning soldiers.

They must have work. The pains and dangers they have endured in our defence give them the right to expect it.

Do you feel justified in holding a job which could be filled by a man who has not only himself to support, but a wife and family as well?

THINK IT OVER

Department of Labour Archives of the Ontario Government.

"You'd think this place had gone mad, parading up and down Yonge Street. Everybody was down on Yonge Street crying, cheering, screaming, women crying, men crying too. Scenes that you don't forget because they don't happen that often. It was just simply glorious. Even I went down there. Factories closed, nobody wanted to work that day."
The Great War and Canadian Society: An Oral History, p. 200.

The joy and relief felt by Canadians at the signing of the Armistice was tempered by the knowledge that 60,000 lives had been lost and many more thousands of people who had gone overseas would never recover fully from the horror they had endured. The deaths and injuries resulting from the Halifax explosion in 1917 and the flu epidemic of 1919, which claimed 50,000 more lives, were further blows to the fabric of Canadian life. World War I resulted in a significant break with traditional values and practices. A way of life had been changed forever. Commentators have spoken of the "lost generation" who could not recreate the world they had known. The communities that had come through the war and to which so many returned from overseas offered a very different society.

Canada in 1919 was profoundly different from the Canada of 1914 in a number of important ways – demographic, economic, political and social. Serious divisions between French and English, between the eastern and western parts of the country, between labour and capital created a climate of uncertainty. Unemployment and inflation increased during the post-war economic slump and labour militancy intensified, culminating in massive walkouts across the nation in the spring of 1919.

Even though women had proven their worth as citizens during the war, and women relatives of service men and those in the service themselves had been granted the vote, when the war was over and large numbers of men returned to Canada, the women were expected to return to their homes and give up their hard-won jobs to returning veterans. Many widows had to support their families, and thousands of other women did not want to return to the home; their wartime experiences had opened their eyes to new possibilities.

Many women strongly objected to the demands to return to the home and give up their places in factories and offices. The attitude toward workingwomen had changed in other ways. It was now acceptable for a young woman to work until she married, since her wages could help with the family expenses. Women's presence in the workforce was tolerated as long as they did not try to take jobs normally reserved for men. Women were strongly encouraged to focus on so-called "women's jobs. More and more women were being employed as sales help in stores, as filing clerks and stenographers in business offices and as factory workers because they could perform such duties as well as men – and they would work for much lower wages.

GREEN DRAGON PRESS

Opportunities expanded for women in nursing and medicine. Female doctors gained wide praise for their work during the war. Some had gained their reputations in hospitals in Canada; others had done so in field hospitals in France.

New freedoms in dress came for several reasons. Women working on the farm and in munitions during the war adopted appropriate clothing. This was out of necessity, as the fabric needed for the war effort took priority. The new fashions in dress and hairstyles suited the new confidence many women had gained as they explored work opportunities that been previously closed to them. Clothes were less constricting and the shorter hairstyles less time consuming.

Opportunities for Black women, however, were limited. Violet Blackman came to Toronto in 1920, almost two years after the end of the war. She described the city and the opportunities for Black women:

"That was 1920; then Toronto was just a village. The streetcars had no sidings to them; you could jump on and off, but they always had the motorman and a conductor on them. The Exhibition Ground and Sunnyside, that was all the lake, and the Union Station – there was nothing but the lake. You couldn't get any position, regardless who you were and how educated you were, other than housework because even if the employer would employ you, those that you had to work with would not work with you."

We're Rooted Here and They Can't Pull Us Up. Dionne Brand et al. p 172,173.

For all the changes and increased opportunities for women, emphasis still remained on the importance of women's role as homemaker. However so many men had died in the conflict that many women lived their lives alone, whether or not they wished to follow the social norm.

In August, 1927, in what has become known as the "Persons Case," Emily Murphy and four Alberta women – Nellie McClung, Henrietta Muir Edwards, Louise McKinney and Irene Parlby, later known as the "Famous Five," – petitioned the Supreme Court of Canada for clarification on women's eligibility for appointment to the Senate. The petition was denied. The five women then took their case to the Judicial Committee of the Privy Council of Great Britain. On October 18, 1929, the Committee ruled Section 24 of the British North America Act should apply equally to women. With that decision women became eligible for nomination to the Senate. One year later, Cairine Reay Wilson was the first woman to take her place in the Senate of Canada. By implication this victory meant that many other fields opened to women.

But even as women gained new rights society would still seek to confine them to the stereotypical "woman's place."

Mass circulation magazines and advice books acknowledged the hopes raised in this new decade by featuring "the girl of the new age," creating the popular notion of the "flapper." On the other hand, there were some doubts about the idea of "the new woman." The end of the Great War had left many Canadians feeling threatened and insecure, and they turned to traditional values and institutions for a sense of stability. Marriage remained the accepted occupation for women, and many magazines offered advice and information on the subject.

The experiences of seven decades of grassroots organizing, speaking, writing and cooperating had created a pool of experienced women reformers ready to cope with the aftermath of the Great War. Though they had deep concerns about the human cost of the war and strong commitment to preventing another, as expressed in the poem *In Flanders Now* by journalist and author Edna Jacques, still they had high hopes for the future.

In Flanders Now

We have kept faith ye Flanders dead,
Sleep well beneath the poppies red
That mark your place,
The torch your dying hands did throw
We held it high before the foe
And answered bitter blow for blow
In Flanders fields.

And where your hero's blood was spilled
The guns are now forever stilled
And silent grown.
There is no cry of tortured pain
And blood will never flow again
In Flanders fields.

Forever hold in our sight
Will be those crosses gleaming white
That guard your sleep
Rest you to peace the task is done
The fight you left us we have won
And peace on earth had just begun

Edna Jacques, *Uphill All the Way*, p. 129.

GREEN DRAGON PRESS

Loss and Remembrance

Soon after the war was over, the governments of the world went about reburying the dead. Those who had been buried quickly while the bombs exploded above were permanently interred in peaceful cemeteries. Monuments were erected, as cities and towns were re-built. Canadian nurses who died were honoured for their courage and sacrifice by the Nursing Sisters' marble Memorial located in the Hall of Honour in the Centre Block on Parliament Hill, and the Cavell monument in downtown Toronto, created by sculptor Florence Wyle.

Annual, sometimes daily, remembrance ceremonies became a part of life – proof that those who survived the Great War would not forget. The poppy - that sturdy flower that decorated the hastily dug graves in Flanders, and survived the ravages of war, soon became a symbol of all that had been lost and accomplished. By 1920, the poppy was officially adopted in the United States. A year later, French widows and orphans were making and selling silk poppies; their profits were going to veterans' families or programs for disabled veterans.

Mary Riter Hamilton

The Canadian War Memorial Fund and the Canadian War Records Office hired official war artists to record Canada's participation in the war. Near the battlefront, the war artists were always male; a few women artists secured commissions to record activity on the home front and to produce portraits of military and political figures. At the end of the war, a magazine called *The Gold Stripe* offered Mary a commission that required her to return to Europe. The magazine, whose proceeds went to the War Amputations Club of British Columbia, hired her to paint the battlefields of Belgium and France. The paintings would appear in *The Gold Stripe*, which published articles and illustrations relating to the war.

In 1919, only six months after the end of the war, Mary returned to Europe. Her special mission was to record the battlefields before all signs of battle were removed. At Vimy, Mary suffered in snow and extreme cold, yet she wrote in one of her letters to *The Gold Stripe* "I want to get the spirit of it…I feel that it is fortunate that I arrived before it is too late to get a real impression."

It took courage for Mary to live in war-torn Europe. Gangs of criminals roamed the countryside, live ammunition littered the battle zones, and her only neighbours were Chinese labourers hired to clear the wasted battlefields. She lived alone in a military hut and the food was often inedible. She was "mighty cold and uncomfortable" she wrote in one letter but in another she stated she would not leave until "I finish the work I have come here to do." And so Mary persisted in her task of producing a unique record of Canada's part in The Great War.

GREEN DRAGON PRESS

The Battlefield Paintings

From 1919 to 1922, Mary produced over three hundred battlefield paintings, many completed on site. She had travelled widely in Europe before the war and must have been deeply moved by the wasteland around her. Her grim, impressionistic paintings bear witness to the lasting horrors of war.

Mary focused on battles where Canadian soldiers had fought and died. Her paintings show ruined buildings, scorched woods, overturned tanks and deserted roads scattered through Europe's ravaged countryside.

Yet, as if to emphasize that Canadian soldiers did not die in vain, some of the paintings hint at new life. Some show flowers growing in the trenches beside no man's land, or ordinary people gathering in markets.

The paintings she produced in 1919 were exhibited in Victoria and Vancouver by the War Amputations Club and the Imperial Order of the Daughters of the Empire. As usual, however, her work received more attention in Europe. In 1922, some of Mary's battlefield paintings were exhibited in the Foyer of the Paris Opera as well as at the Société des Artistes, the Société Nationale des Beaux-Arts, and at the Somme Memorial Exhibition held in Amiens, France. At the Somme Memorial Exhibition, Mary was awarded the purple ribbon of Les Palmes Académiques, the Order of Public Instruction. Her award was as high a distinction as a woman could receive in France at the time. In 1923, over a hundred of her battlefield paintings were exhibited in London, England. While in Europe Mary received a number of offers to purchase her collection, but she refused. She had other plans for her battlefield paintings.

Mary donated 227 of her paintings to Canada's Public Archives, as a memorial to Canadians who died in the war. Unfortunately, in spite of the attention received in Europe and the generosity of her gift, she received little attention. She was forgotten by the world and she died in poverty in 1954.

HERstory II: Women of Canada's Past, by Susan Merritt.
Reprinted by permission.

GREEN DRAGON PRESS

Looking to the Future

By 1920, Canadian women would experience a world very different from that which their mothers and grandmothers had known. Partly through the contributions they had made to the war effort, and partly through the dedicated campaigning of the suffragists, Canadian women had made some substantial gains in their struggle for equality of status.

Agnes Campbell Macphail of Ontario became the first woman elected to the House of Commons in 1921. Nellie McClung won a seat in Alberta the same year, becoming the third woman to sit in that province's legislature. Later in the decade, great female athletes like Ethel Catherwood and Bobby Rosenfield won Olympic gold medals for Canada.

First Woman Member of Parliament Agnes Macphail - 1921

A teacher in rural Ontario before running for election, Macphail was the first woman elected to the House of Commons in 1921, representing the riding of Grey South East as an independent, keeping close links with the United Farmers of Ontario party. Macphail was an ardent feminist and an advocate of social change and devoted most of her life to public service at a time when women were not welcomed in the public arena. Defeated federally in 1940, she moved to Toronto to become a newspaper columnist and in 1943 was nominated as the CCF candidate in the provincial riding of York East and won, thus becoming one of the first two women elected to the provincial legislature. She worked for women, miners and prisoners, founded the Canadian branch of the Elizabeth Fry Society and was largely responsible for Ontario's first pay equity legislation in 1951. Macphail was never afraid to speak her mind. Along with Nellie McClung she was noted for her pithy, quotable comments. One example:

"That seems to be the haunting fear of mankind – that the advancement of women will some time, some way, some place, interfere with some man's comfort." Agnes Macphail.

GREEN DRAGON PRESS

The Persons Case

"It would be absurd to ask a woman today if she thought of herself as a person."
Ontario Women's Directorate – **Moments in History, 1992.**

"...and to those who ask why the word [person] should include females, the answer is,
why should it not?"
Lord Sankey, Lord Chancellor of the Privy Council, London, England October 18, 1929

The 1920s ended on a note of triumph for women's rights with the winning of the Persons Case in 1929, which established by reinterpreting the word "person" in Section 24 of the British North America Act that women were eligible for appointment to the Canadian Senate. Although the campaign started in 1927, its roots reach back to 1916 when Emily Murphy had just been created the first woman police magistrate within the British Empire. During her first day as a judge an enraged defence lawyer told her that she was not a "person" under the British North America Act and therefore had no right to be holding court anyway. In 1919 the first conference of the Federated Women's Institute of Canada sent a resolution requesting the prime minister to appoint a woman to the Senate. Other powerful women's organizations followed suit, but they were told that the nomination of a woman was impossible without an amendment to the BNA Act. In 1927, Emily Murphy, with Nellie McClung, Irene Parlby, Louise McKinney and Henrietta Muir Edwards, petitioned the Supreme Court asking for an interpretation on just who were "persons." Their question was "Does the word Persons in Section 24 of the British North America Act, 1967, include female persons?" The argument was heard in the Supreme Court of Canada on March 14, 1928. The verdict came five weeks later and was a bitter

disappointment for the petitioners. The court ruled against them. The five Supreme Court justices decided that the BNA Act must be construed in the light of what was intended in 1867, when no woman was enfranchised in Canada, and that therefore women were not eligible for appointment to the Senate.

"The question being understood to be "Are Women eligible for appointment to the Senate of Canada" the question is answered in the negative."

April 28, 1928 Supreme Court of Canada Decision. Archives of Canada

After a year during which the five appellants hoped that the government would introduce a motion to amend the BNA Act, they decided to appeal to the Judicial Committee of the Privy Council in London, England. Finally, on October 18, 1929, Lord Sankey, the Lord Chancellor read the decision at Temple Bar.

Their Lordships have come to the conclusion that the word persons includes members of the male and female sex and that therefore the question propounded by the Governor General must be answered in the affirmative, and that women are eligible to be summoned and become members of the Senate of Canada.

And further declared that:

"The exclusion of women from all public offices is a relic of days more barbarous than ours."

The Privy Council decision was indeed a huge victory for the women of Canada. Those who wanted to enter politics could now be appointed to the Senate. But that did not mean women would have an easy time finding their way into Parliament's Upper Chamber, because although laws had changed, attitudes had not. The ensuing decades, the Great Depression of the Thirties followed by World War II would once again change Canadian society and challenge Canadian women in ways that no one could ever have imagined....

GREEN DRAGON PRESS

Selected Activities

Chapter 1: On the Home Front

Knowledge and Understanding

View the National Film Board film about women in factories during World War I - "And We Knew How to Dance." Make a list of the contributions these Ontario working women made during the war. (www.nfb.ca) Pretend you were one of the women in the film. Write a letter to a friend in another town, telling her about your adventure.

Thinking, Inquiring, Communicating

Poster: To the Women of Canada. As a class, discuss the probable impact of World War I propaganda on women. Compare the messages or images (or both) presented in the poster and explain why there are significant differences.

Have students imagine they are one of the women of the time, and create diary entries about their reaction to posters.

Research

Compare World War I and World War II propaganda posters.

Ada Kelly: Read and discuss the letter of recommendation. You might want to raise such questions as: The principal implied that there might be a problem hiring a Black woman to teach for the Board. Do you think his concern was justified? Why? Do you think the principal placed too much emphasis on Ada's personal appearance? Does this have any relationship with her ability as a teacher?

Applying Knowledge

Have each student create a page in an imaginary diary in which Ada Kelly records her teaching experiences. See Resources for sources on early 20th century teaching.

Write and perform a skit – a day in the life of a factory worker.

Hattie Rhu Hatchett. In groups, write the music and lyrics for a song about female factory or farm workers.

GREEN DRAGON PRESS

Chapter 2: The Fight for the Vote

Knowledge and Understanding

As a class, discuss the meaning of disenfranchisement.

As a class decide on a social/equity issue that you feel should be addressed at your school. Create a petition and circulate it within the school. Research where to send the petition.

Thinking, Inquiring, Communicating

Opinions differ regarding the granting of the vote. Initially Canadian women in the military, and women relatives of men serving in the military, received the right to vote. Later it was granted to other Canadians, but not all women. Some historians see granting the first franchise as a cynical attempt to gain votes for the Union Party, guaranteeing that the Conscription Act would pass. Others say that the vote was an acknowledgment of women's support of the war effort. Still others say that the franchise was an inevitable outcome of the years of work by suffrage groups. Have students discuss these different views, and support one of them, giving reasons for their opinion.

Research

Individual research: What rights, if any, did woman have during this time? Property? Parental? Did all women, regardless of race or colour, hold these rights?

Research the life of Nellie McClung.

Using the documents in this chapter and other research, create a chart with two columns. In column one, list the arguments against women's suffrage. In column two, in your own words, comment on the logic of the arguments. Do the same with the arguments for women's suffrage.

Applying Knowledge

Re-enact the Mock Parliament (see main introduction). Imagine that the women of the Manitoba Equality League had access to contemporary technology (fax, email, internet, text messaging). How would their strategies have been different? In what ways? Valentine greetings post card: This post card shows one public view of the issue of votes for women. Analyze the image. Create a pro-suffrage satirical post card.

Chapter 3: Far From Home

Knowledge and Understanding

Discuss 1918 article: Nurses Disdain Death to help Wounded Men. Did you know that Canadian nurses were killed in World War I? Use the headline as an opening discussion for other questions such as: Was Canada bombed during World War I? What do you think the reaction was in Canada to this article?

Using *The War Diaries of Clare Gass* or *Nobody Ever Wins a War: The War Diaries of Ella Mae Bongard*, create letters from family members to Clare or Ella Mae.

Thinking, Inquiring, Communicating

Very little has been written about women in the military during World War I. What might be some of the reasons for this?

How can letters and diaries help historians understand the roles women played during the war?

How do these documents provide important historical information for Canada?

Research

Individual research: Read letters written by nurses during World War I and World War II and compare and contrast them.

Class project: Do further research on Canadian Nursing Sisters during the war.

Applying Knowledge

Create "letters to the editor" in response to the article Nurses Disdain Death to help Wounded Men.

Using *The War Diaries of Clare Gass* or *Nobody Ever Wins a War: The War Diaries of Ella Mae Bongard*, discuss a typical day of a military nurse.

GREEN DRAGON PRESS

Chapter 4: Afterword

Knowledge and Understanding

In groups, make a list on chart paper of all the important roles women played during the war and explain how their contribution was essential in the war effort both at home and overseas. Compare your results and find common themes.

Thinking, Inquiring, Communicating

Discuss in class whether you think it was fair that women were pressured to give up their jobs to make room for returning veterans. Could there have been a solution that was more equitable?

What do you think happened to the fruit pickers, factory workers, nurses and ambulance drivers after the war?

Research

Research the life of sculptor Florence Wyle, the artist who depicted women contributing to the war effort at home and who created the monument honouring Edith Cavell and serving nursing sisters.

Compare Edna Jacques' poem *In Flanders Now* with the original *In Flander's Fields* by John McCrae. What are the differences?

Applying Knowledge

Create a bulletin board display on women's contributions to the war effort. You could arrange the board by themes such as work in the war factories, nursing, and activities on the home front. Include pictures, maps and letters.

A recent story by local historian Douglas Mackey* of Powassan, Ontario suggests that John McCrae actually gave the original copy of the poem *In Flanders Fields* to Jean Cameron, the nurse who was looking after him, and not, as depicted in the television Heritage Minute, to a soldier standing nearby. In groups, write the story-board for a new Heritage Minute describing John McCrae handing the poem to Jean Cameron.

* www.pastforward.ca/perspectives/September for story by Douglas Mackey.

Design a monument honouring women who served at home and abroad.

What other ways can Canadians honour these women?

GREEN DRAGON PRESS

Selected Resources

Books:

Agnes Macphail and the Politics of Equality. Terry Crowley. Toronto: J. Lorimer, 1992.

Canada's Nursing Sisters. G.W.L. Nicholson. Ottawa: Canadian War Museum, 1975.

Canadian Women: A History. Alison Prentice et al. Toronto: Harcourt Brace Jovanovich, 1988.

Firing the Heather: The Life & Times of Nellie McClung. Mary Hallett & Marilyn Davis. Saskatoon: Fifth House, 1993.

HERstoryII: Women from Canada's Past. Susan Merritt. Toronto: Vanwell Press, 1995.

HERStory III: Women from Canada's Past. Susan Merritt. Toronto: Vanwell Press, 1999.

On All Frontiers: Four Centuries of Canadian Nursing. Editors: Christina Bates, Dianne Dodd, and Nicole Rousseau. Ottawa: University of Ottawa Press, 2005.

The Great War & Canadian Society: An Oral History. Edited by Daphne Read. New Hogtown Press, Toronto, 1978.

The War Diaries of Clare Gass. Edited by Susan Mann. Montreal: McGill Queens University Press, 2000.

Nobody Ever Wins a War: The World War I Diaries of Ella Mae Bongard, R.N. Edited by Eric Scott. Ottawa, 1997. Distributed by Green Dragon Press.

Rilla of Ingleside. Lucy Maude Montgomery. Toronto: McClelland & Stewart. [1921]. 1973.

Spotlight Canada. J. Bradley Cruxton & W. Douglas Wilson. Don Mills: Oxford University Press, 2000.

Tapestry of War: A Private View of Canadians in the Great War. Sandra Gwynn. Toronto: HarperCollins, 1993.

The Woman Suffrage Movement in Canada, 2nd ed. Catherine L. Cleverdon. Toronto: University of Toronto Press, 1974.

Women at Work, 1850-1930. Janice Acton, Penny Goldsmith & Bonnie Shepard, eds. Toronto: Canadian Women's Educational Press, 1974.

GREEN DRAGON PRESS

Videos:

In Flanders Fields.
<u>Viewer Plus</u>: 1-866-663-0262

Angels of Mercy: Nursing Sisters in World War I and II.
<u>Sound Venture</u>: 613-241-5010

And We Knew How to Dance
<u>National Film Board</u>: www.nfb.ca

No Man's Land (Mary Riter Hamilton)
<u>War Amps</u> 1-800-250-3030

Websites:

www.valourandhorror.com/DB/ISSUE/Women/Women

www.vac-acc.gc.ca: Veterans Affairs Canada

www.waramps.ca

www.vac-acc.gc.ca: Veterans Affairs Canada

www.coolwomen.org "Women Take the Right to Vote"

www.thecanadianencyclopedia.com/index Monuments, World Wars I and II

www.pastforward.ca/perspectives/September_152006.htm Jean Cameron

Poster:

Four Centuries of Canadian Nursing. Toronto: Green Dragon Press, 2005.
www3sympatico.ca/equity.greendragonpress

GREEN DRAGON PRESS